1983

CENSORS AND SOCIAL CONFLICT IN THE SPANISH THEATRE

The Case of Alfonso Sastre

W9-ADC-091

T. Avril Bryan

UNIVERSITY
PRESS OF
AMERICA

Dedication

To my husband Anthony.

iii

Acknowledgements

I wish to express my gratitude to Professor
Richard W. Tyler of the University of Nebraska-Lincoln
for the many suggestions that he made with respect to
this manuscript. In addition the Department of
Language and Linguistics of the University of the West
Indies at St. Augustine made the preparation of this
manuscript possible. I also gratefully acknowledge
the assistance of the University of the West Indies
in meeting part of the publication costs of this
manuscript. Finally my thanks to Patricia Mannette
for the typing of the manuscript.

TABLE OF CONTENTS

PREFACE

Alfonso Sastre is perhaps one of the most controversial dramatists of contemporary Spain. This controversy arose not only because of the nature of his plays which often offended the censors; but also because of his political beliefs and his wife's political activities.

In 1974 his wife, psychologist Genoneva Forest was implicated in the assassination of Spain's Premier, Admiral Luis Carrero Blanco, and was consequently imprisoned. Because of the legal complications, Sastre too was imprisoned for months and since his release in 1975 has been relatively quiet concerning his dramatic output.

The reasons for the controversy over Sastre the man and dramatist is fully explored in this work. In attempting to understand and fully appreciate his theatre one is immediately faced with the problems which he encountered with official censorship. In addition, the firm view held by Sastre with respect to the important role which society plays in the life of the individual deserves detailed examination. His drama is primarily social in content and outlook, and in various critical essays, Sastre outlines his theories on the relationship between society and drama. These theories are analyzed. So also is the individual's role in the society taking into consideration the importance of the family. Both Sastre and his wife are social activists and in many ways it can be said that his dramas have become a reflection of his own life and that of his family.

CHAPTER I

ALFONSO SASTRE: DRAMATIST AND ACTIVIST

Alfonso Sastre, the dramatist and man of letters, has proved to be a controversial figure in the contemporary Spanish theatre. He has been attacked and praised, defended and scorned. Yet, he has continued his dramatic production and has attempted to defend his position in numerous articles. Because of these diametrically opposed opinions, Sastre has been the subject of various scholarly articles concerning both his theatre and his essays. He is perhaps the most discussed Spanish dramatist of contemporary Spain. One critic has even suggested that the name of Alfonso Sastre is better known than his theatre--at least in Spain--since Sastre is an author who "ha sabido llevar su voz de protesta y disconformidad más allá de los ámbitos específicos de su dedicación literaria...y que su obra dramática no ha encontrado los cauces oportunos para su libre y normal expresión en los escenarios."[1]

It is no surprise that Sastre's imprisonment caused great concern internationally in both political and literary circles. Sastre and his wife, psychologist Genoveva Forest, were imprisioned in the fall of 1974 by Spanish authorities for crimes against the state allegedly committed by Genoveva. Sastre's wife was implicated in bomb explosions in Madrid, accused of active involvement with Basque terrorists and charged with murder in the assassination of Premier Admiral Luis Carrero Blanco in December 1973. Under Spanish law a husband is legally responsible for crimes committed by his wife.[2] Consistently there have been attacks waged against Sastre, the playwright, in order to undermine his prestige.

Why has the author become a topic of controversy? The debate over Sastre is related directly to the state of the contemporary Spanish theatre. Scholars are generally in agreement that the Spanish theatre has been in a state of crisis since the Civil War, though there is much debate over the reasons for this critical situation. The blame for this prolonged crisis ranges from the economy to the audience. Rising costs during the fifties and sixties prohibited many a theatrical production as well as the admission of many an interested spectator. It cost far less to go to the cinema and

1

this attracted audiences away from the theatre. The intellectual rarely attended the theatre while the bourgeoisie delegated the choice of entertainment to the newspaper critic who is the catalyst of theatrical success in Spain.[3] Many legitimate theatres closed their doors because of increasing mass entertainment such as football and the movies. Public indifference also contributed to the problem. Newspaper critics, rather than scholarly or literary critics, have dictated and continue to dictate, their theatrical opinion to a susceptible bourgeoisie who seem to favor foreign plays.

Of the Spanish plays which were being performed in the fifties and sixties, a substantial difference existed between a prize-winning play and a play worthy of being presented. The receipt of a _premio_ did not guarantee excellence.[4] On the other hand, a play such as Sastre's _Escuadra hacia la muerte_, which merited and received warm acclaim by critics and the theatre-going public alike, was curtailed after only three performances in 1953, for censorship reasons. Although the theatre in its various aspects was quite active, rigid censorship presented a difficult obstacle for many writers and prohibited the performance of the works of some dramatists such as García Lorca.[5]

Such difficulties notwithstanding, writers still continued to contribut to the Spanish drama. A plethora of theatrical works exists, be they good, bad or indifferent. Some critics fear that a profusion of dramatic creations signifies theatrical decadence. Others are quich to ascertain that the theatre is not completely decrepit. George Wellwarth points out that very often the good plays, particularly those which would be termed controversial by the censors, were excluded from the theatre. Nevertheless, many Spanish dramatists continued to write good plays and refused to be discouraged by the severe censorship. Their plays are termed "underground drama" or censored drama and there are many dramatists whose works and names (unlike those of Buero, Sastre, Olmo and Muñoz) are still unknown to the general public.[6] Largely, they were unable to have their works published and performed, except perhaps for one night performances. Both publishers and producers were reluctant to print or produce these plays if there was the possibility that they could be prohibited by the censors. Many very good plays remain unpublished and unproduced in Spain.

What then are the types of plays which continue to

be produced in Spain? A large number of foreign plays
are performed. Alfonso Sastre himself has provided
translations and adaptations of non-Spanish dramas. In
addition to the historical and the social satires of
the pre-Civil War era, the most popularly acclaimed
drama has been the "theatre of evasion" and the more
serious "theatre of commitment". Antonio Buero Vallejo
and Alfonso Sastre are clearly the leaders of the latter type of genre. The "theatre of commitment" is characterized by the contemporary problems which are presented, and by the relationship of the dramatist's political views to art. This is a theatre of protest
and outrage with a message which has to be presented in
a special manner.[7] A further trait of this drama is
its open ending wherein the playwright withholds any
solution to the problem. Since no dialectical solution
is expected the intention is to produce a catharsis in
the spectator which causes one to agonize over a possible solution. This is what Sastre terms a "theatre
of anguish" and one which he advocates above all others.
Francis Donahue points out that the Spanish dramatists
do not seek to present works with the same philosophical structure as Jean-Paul Sartre, although the strain
of existential anguish is clearly apparent, particularly in the works of Alfonso Sastre.[8] After a subjective
reflection of the play, the spectator is expected to
draw his own conclusions. The vehicle for this kind of
theatre is obviously tragedy. Sastre asserts that "el
espectador de la tragedia no busca el sufrimiento;
acepta la mortificación. El expectador se siente mere-
cidamente mortificado. Acepta la tortura en un movimi-
ento de autocastigo. Entonces, ¿es que se siente cul-
pable? Sí, la tragedia despierta en él un profundo
sentimiento de culpabilidad. ¿Y...? Acepta ser mortificado. ¿Y después? Cuando la tragedia termina su
espíritu ha sido purificado. ¿Y después? Después--a
veces--una revolución social. O, por lo menos, un so-
corro social. Entonces, ¿resulta que la tragedia era
otra cosa?"[9]

Sastre, who was born in 1926, participated in 1945
in the formation of a group called Arte Nuevo--an experimental theatre group. It was composed largely of university students and constituted an attempt to respond
to the crisis in the Spanish theatre. The group lasted
two years during which Sastre wrote two one act plays
Uranio 235 and Cargamento de sueños. Also, he colla-
borated with Medardo Fraile to write Ha sonado la muerte
and Comedia sonámbula. After the dissolution of this

group, Sastre continued to write plays and articles.
In 1950, together with José María de Quinto, he announced the founding of a new theatre group called Teatro de Agitación Social (T.A.S.). In October of that year the group published a manifesto in which it proposed to represent a total vision of society and not simply to be a theatre of the proletariat. The members denied that they were politicians and affirmed that they were men of the theatre who were willing to take the "agitation" to all spheres of Spanish life. They reaffirmed the fact that theatre is a social art: a) because the theatre cannot be reduced to the aesthetic contemplation of a refined minority and b) that because of this projection, the theatre can no longer be merely artistic. The intent of the manifesto was to propel the public once more to the theatre. Before these ideals could be implemented the group became the victim of official pressure.

In a further response to the crisis in the Spanish theatre Sastre together with José María de Quinto and other notable figures, issued a list of criteria in 1955 which they found to be essential in overcoming the current problems of the Spanish theatre.[10] First they stated what they considered as reasons for the decadence: the increased popularity and superior organization of the cinema, more keenly felt in Spain than in other countries of Europe; and the insufficient and anachronistic theatrical management. Among the solutions offered by the group were the creation of small theatres giving daily performances under the direction of responsible theatre people; assistance from the State in the formation of National Theatres; the withholding of national prizes if there were no works which merited them; legal sanction for works in place of the current censorship; the teaching of the theatre as an art form in Spain; various measures for capturing new audiences; an appeal to theatre critics to consider deeply the artistic and social importance of the performance; and the necessity to propagandize the Spanish theatre abroad. Finally, the group declared its faith in the realization of these goals while maintaining that a "Theatre of Political and Social Preoccupation" was definitely possible.

During this period Sastre witnessed the performance of his play La mordaza, which was directed by his friend and colleague Quinto, and saw the publication of Drama y sociedad, his first collection of critical essays. In 1960 Sastre and Quinto ventured once more to form yet another theatrical group. This time it was called the Grupo de Teatro Realista (G.T.R.). Again, the

purpose of the G.T.R. was to revitalize the Spanish
theatre but its format was more refined and precise
than that of the T.A.S. In the declaration issued by
Sastre and Quinto concerning the G.T.R.,[11] they asser-
ted that the intention was to intervene in the course
of the Spanish theatre in a most energetic and overt
manner. The general pattern of their work was to be a
theoretical and practical investigation into the various forms of realism. The G.T.R. was also to attend
to the training of new actors and to the study of stage
techniques and interpretation. A relationship was also
established with UNESCO'S International Institute of
Theatre as well as with colleagues and publications in
Europe and America. Five years after the formation of
the G.T.R. Sastre's Anatomía del realismo was published.
This was yet another collection of critical essays which
reflected his intense interest in realism. The G.T.R.
was also largely responsible for the stage production
of Sastre's En la red; but as with the other two previous theatrical groups, the activities of this organization were soon curtailed because of difficulties with
finances and the censors.

As previously mentioned, Sastre's dramatic career
was initiated in 1964 with the writing of Ha sonado la
muerte. During the periods in which Sastre participated
in the founding of the theatrical groups discussed above
he continued his dramatic output. To date, the plays
which he has written, including adaptations, fall into
different categories corresponding to the dramatic ideas
and theories of the artist. The first four one act plays
written during the period of the Arte Nuevo group are
all experimental in form. Around 1950 Sastre began to
explore the social aspect of the theatre. One critic
sees three different stages in the development of
Sastre's published theatre: 1) a drama of experimenta-
tion, 2) a drama of social agitation and 3) a drama of
investigation.[12] Another, Farris Anderson, defines two
major categories with respect to the image of man
portrayed: 1) dramas of frustration and 2) dramas of
possibility.[13] He further subdivides the second category with respect to the dramatic forms and techniques
utilized according to: a) dramas of social realism and
b) the epic drama, which includes four unpublished plays.
Anderson sees the dramas of frustration as plays in
which the characters are overwhelmed by their circumstances and no solutions are offered to them. In this
group he classfies Ha sonado la muerte, 1946, Uranio
235, 1946, Cargamento de sueños, 1946, Comedia sonámbula,
1947, Ana Kleiber, 1955, La sangre de Dios, 1955 and

5

El cuervo, 1956. The dramas of frustration are still essentially experimental in ·form. Various elements such as dreams, flashbacks with fundamental distortions of time and space, long narrative reports and the appearance of the author himself in the drama, give "dramatic form to the senseless world implicit in these dramas."[14] In the second category, the dramas of social realism include Prólogo patético, 1950, El cubo de la basura, 1951, Escuadra hacia la muerte, 1952, El pan de todos, 1953, La mordaza, 1954, Tierra roja, 1954, Guillermo Tell tiene los ojos tristes, 1955, Muerte en el barrio, 1955, En la red, 1959, La cornada, 1959, and Oficio de tinieblas, 1962. The second group of this category includes Asalto nocturno, 1959, as an antecedent and four unpublished plays, La sangre y la ceniza La taberna fantástica, El banquete and Crónicas romanas.[15]

In all the dramas of possibility, the individual has an open path to a solution if he decides to exercise his voluntad and proceed from inertia to action. The protagonists must act in order to give meaning to their existence. Through their initiative they are able to transform the existing circumstance even though the results of their action may cause pain, suffering and grief. There is opportunity to improve one's lot in life or rather in the society.

The dramas of social realism or social agitation reflect Sastre's profound concern with the role of society in the theatre. They are based on the Aristotelian concept of tragedy. Sastre deliberately chose tragedy as the vehicle for his ideas and techniques. In his conception of tragedy and drama, he views tragedy as something durable. "Hay, pues, en la tragedia algo permanente: su sustancia metafísica; algo permanente, pero dotado de plasticidad: la forma artística, y algo corruptible; lo que llega a la tragedia por ser ésta, en cada momento, una función social."[16] Another dimension to this concept is apparent in Sastre's statement that a drama is something like a tragedy "pero con menos sangre, con menos gritos, con un lenguaje más llano, con personajes más vulgares, con expresiones menos turbulentas, con un tono de voz más apagado, con un final sin muerte o con una muerte no muy aparatosa."[17] Although Sastre affirms that there are different kinds of drama, he defines tragedy as what endures when everything unreal including laughter has been decimated: "nos hemos quedado con algo real, punzante".[18] In fact Sastre's concept of tragedy is closely aligned to that in

6

Aristotle's Poetics. He admits that the basis for Drama y sociedad was in fact the work of this Greek master.[19] Thus, for Sastre, tragedy "es una representación lúcida de la existencia humana".[20] It is not merely a drama of good and evil. Tragedy has a perpetuity which melodrama does not. The guilty party is not clearly visible in tragedy, consequently the spectator leaves the performance racked by doubts and questions for which the author has supplied no answers. Sastre's remaining ideas concerning tragedy and drama are directly related to his complex concept of drama and society.

The epic phase in Sastre's dramatic development is marked by the influence of Bertolt Brecht's epic theatre and the Marxist view of literature. Among the collection of essays published in Anatomía del realismo there is one entitled "Posición ante Brecht" in which Sastre explains his view on the epic theatre. He finds everything in Brecht to be admirable except for his theatre. In fact he finds everything indisputable except for Brecht's dramatic theories. The Brechtian characteristic is one of social commitment with an equally aloof detachment and emotional uninvolvement. The result of this is a "disconcerting complexity of tone which is assisted by the apparently clumsy loose textured structure of the 'epic' style".[21] Moelwyn Merchant further proffers that Brecht's most valuable contribution toward any examination of contemporary thinking lies in the "moral and dramatic dilemmas inherent in this ironic counterposing of involvement and detachment".[22]

The consistent exigency of Brechtian theatre, that the spectator should be mentally but not emotionally involved, is questioned by Sastre. But Sastre's greatest disagreement with Brecht is in the phase of interpretation which calls for special techniques on the part of the actor such as that of creating a distance, an alienation between himself and the character he portrays. The epic actor is a narrator of history not of dramatic narrative. Sastre also disapproves of the scenario employed by Brecht--seemingly alien surroundings. Furthermore, Sastre rejects the Brechtian theatre because of its prime concern with real space-time which for him (Sastre) implies the unreality of dramatic space-time.[23] Sastre avoids any identification with current space by utilizing varied geographic locations in his plays. Regardless of locale, the themes which he treats are universal. Sastre contends that to accept unconditionally the dramatic theories of Brecht would mean the

death of drama, since Brecht's theatre corresponds to
the future and the time has not yet arrived for Brecht's
epic theatre. Sastre firmly believes that the real task
for the dramatist lies in the dialectic negation of the
Brechtian negation.[24]

The underlying purpose of Sastre's epic theatre is
to demonstrate the possibility of change in society. He
utilizes most of Brecht's techniques but his "attempt
to surpass Brecht in the creation of a powerful revolutionary theatre is embodied in his persistent use of
shock treatment in sound, light and scenic effects."[25]
Sastre's epic phase is his latest. Anderson insists that
this phase does not signify a contradiction of Sastre's
thought but rather another stage in the dialectical development which has characterized the playwright's work.

A most interesting facet of Sastre the artist is
revealed in his polemic with Buero Vallejo concerning
the "posibilismo o imposibilismo" of drama. That this
polemic took place at all is a direct result of Sastre's
problems with censorship. Sastre has on several occasions criticized the kind of censorship which exists in
Spain. He claims that in its present form it is a public
and private shame.[26] He maintains, together with Quinto,
that it is not a question of a reluctance to acknowledge
social vigilance but rather it should be consistent and
legitimate. At the beginning of the Franco regime,
censorship was more rigid than it is today. Censorship
was previously enforced by a censorship office composed
largely of priests who prohibited anything that offended
the Church, State, or rigid morality.[27] This continued
until 1963 when a censorship committee was formed. The
inconsistencies in this committee's judgments often left
the artists without any solid guidelines to follow.

Sastre is but one of many dramatists who continued
to experience difficulty in getting their works published and performed. What is deplorable is that his works
continued to be prohibited without any specific explanation. A work rejected on one occasion might be approved
on another. In addition to the censorship problem,
Sastre has had to face at times the public's disinterest
in and dislike for his plays. This same public continues to applaud Buero Vallejo when, as one critic so aptly
phrases it, "the intellectual, moral and political inten-
tions of the two are very similar".[28] The means of
communication employed by Sastre is different. Buero's
success with the public merely indicates the extent to

which certain sections of Spanish society (largely the bourgeoisie) are predisposed to receive his message. Sastre has been criticized for "defects" which are also apparent in the works of others: a lack of poetry, an ideological partisanship and a rather brusque style of writing.[29]

Buero's work can be characterized as a tragedy of hope, while that of Sastre can be termed a tragedy of anguish. The two theories of tragedy concern the possibility of an open versus a closed situation.[30] Buero's theatre reflects the possibility of escape from the final catastrophe born out of the hope to act in a given situation. It is a negation of despair. Sastre tried to refute this in his criticism of Buero's theatre in which he accused Buero of being a conformist. Buero, on the other hand criticized those dramatists who write "impossible theatre", knowing that it would be prohibited and that the result would be an increase particularly in foreign publicity.[31] Sastre replied that no theatre is eternally "impossible", perhaps it may be so momentarily, but sooner or later all theatre becomes possible. Thus the concept of "imposibilismo" is invalid. Sastre affirms that some of his so-called impossible dramas were performed eventually and that furthermore this subject only relates to the social-political element and not to the aesthetic-poetic.

Sastre has been consistent in the defense of his theatre and refuses to make any concessions to what has been termed "three redoutable obstacles: censorship, impresarios with a box office complex and a naive public".[32] Pérez Minik has pointed out that Sastre is even hated by some commercial companies of the Madrid stage-- at least he is accepted very reluctantly--while the experimental or "private" theatres perform his works with extraordinary devotion.[33] Perhaps this may explain why so few of his plays have been performed in Spain and perhaps why his latest plays have never been published.

Sastre has continued to write plays as recently as 1971; although the majority of those written since 1963 have not been published. Obviously Sastre believes in his vocation and in his mission as a dramatist. The fact that he has continued his dramatic output, in spite of such obstacles, is commendable. His persistence is to be admired and it must certainly be a source of inspiration to the host of younger writers who continue to produce "underground" drama.

Sastre's theatre appeals to Spanish youth and his works continue to be translated and performed in other parts of Europe and in America. It has been suggested that if Sastre were to utilize the dramatic material which exists in contemporary society, and were to reject any literary material, he might yet become the most important dramatist of contemporary Spain.[34] Sastre's good will to restore some of the lost dignity to the Spanish theatre has been universally recognized. It is with the effort of a new generation of writers, with Buero and Sastre as forerunners, that Spanish drama once more has become truly international.

[1]Ricardo Doménech, "Notas de bibliografía teatral" Cuadernos Hispanoamericanos, 233 (May 1969), p.470.

[2]See Barbara Probst Solomon, "Torture in Spain," The New York Times, 25 November, 1974.

[3]Ignacio Soldevila Durante, "Sobre el teatro español de los últimos veinticinco años", Cuadernos Americanos 22, 1(enero-febrero 1963), 258.

[4]Juan R. Castellano, "Los premios nacionales de teatro en España," Hispania 38, 3(September 1955), 291-293.

[5]Cyrus DeCoster, "The Theatrical Season in Madrid 1945 - 55," Hispania 39, 2(May 1956), 185.

[6]George Wellwarth, Spanish Underground Drama, (University Park, Pennsylvania: Pennsylvania State University Press 1972), p. 5.

[7]See Francis Donahue, "Spain's Theater of Commitment," Books Abroad, 43, 3(Summer 1969), 354-58.

[8]Ibid., 355.

[9]Alfonso Sastre, Drama y sociedad (Madrid: Ediciones Taurus, 1956), p. 97.

[10]Alfonso Sastre, José María de Quinto et al. "Coloquios sobre problemas actuales del teatro en España, "in Alfonso Sastre, Teatro, ed. José Monleón (Madrid: Ediciones Taurus, 1964), pp.101-06.

[11]See "Declaración del G.T.R." in Alfonso Sastre,Teatro, pp. 115-116. The manifesto was first published in Primer Acto, 16 (Sept.-Oct. 1960), n.p. In addition, the production of the first season of the G.T.R. gave rise to another published document "G.T.R.--Primera temporada" Primer Acto, 23 (mayo 1961), pp. 12-18.

[12]Elbert E. Bilyeu, "Alfonso Sastre: An Analysis of his Dramas through 1960," Diss. University of Colorado. 1968, p. 100.

[13]Farris Anderson, Alfonso Sastre, (New York: Twayne Publishers Inc., 1971), pp. 70-71.

[14]Ibid., p. 71.

[15]Ibid., Anderson has studied the manuscripts of the four unpublished plays and has discussed them in an article "The New Theatre of Alfonso Sastre," Hispania, 55, 4 (Dec. 1972), 840-847. They will be omitted from this study.

[16]Drama y sociedad, p. 22.

[17]Ibid., p. 13.

[18]Ibid., p. 17.

[19]See the "Prefacio" of Anatomía del realismo, (Barcelona: Ediciones Seix Barral, S.A., 1965), p. 7.

[20]Drama y sociedad, p. 33.

[21]See W. Moelwyn Merchant "The irony of Bertolt Brecht" in Man in the Modern Theatre ed. Nathan A. Scott Jr., (Richmond, Virginia: John Knox Press, 1965), p. 60.

[22]Ibid., p. 62.

[23]See Kessel Schwartz, "Tragedy and the Crticism of Alfonso Sastre," Symposium 21, 4 (Winter 1967), 338-346. This article was also reproduced in a collection of articles published by Professor Schwartz in The Meaning ofExistence in Contemporary Hispanic Literature, (Coral Gables, Florida: University of Miami Press, 1969), pp. 162-70.

[24]Alfonso Sastre, "Primeras notas para un encuentro con Bertolt Brecht", Primer Acto, 13, (marzo-abril 1959), p. 13.
In addition see Anatomía del realismo, p. 48, 68.

[25]Anderson, "The New Theatre of Alfonso Sastre", p. 841.

[26]"Documento sobre el teatro español", Alfonso Sastre, Teatro, pp. 117-123.

[27]Patricia W. O'Connor, "Government censorship in the Contemporary Spanish Theatre", Educational Theater Journal 18, 4 (Dec. 1960), 443-49.

[28]Domingo Pérez Minik, "Se trata de Alfonso Sastre, Dramaturgo melancólico de la Revolución", Alfonso Sastre, Teatro, pp. 11-36.

[29]Ibid.

[30]Kessel Schwartz, "Posibilismo and Imposibilismo: The Buero Vallejo-Sastre Polemic", Homenaje a Frederico de Onís (1885-1966), Revista Hispánica Moderna 34 (1968), 436-45.

[31]For full details of this polemic concerning "posibilismo" and "imposibilismo", see the following articles: Alfonso Sastre, "Teatro imposible y pacto social", Primer Acto, 14 (mayo-junio 1960), pp. 1-2; Antonio Buero Vallejo, "Obligada precisión acerca del imposibilismo", Primer Acto 15 (julio-agosto 1960), pp. 1-6; Alfonso Sastre, "A modo de respuesta, Primer Acto, 16 (sept.-oct. 1960), pp. 1-2; Anatomía del realismo, pp. 76-77; Rafael Vázquez Zamora, "Alfonso Sastre no acepta el 'posibilismo'", Insula, Año 15, 164-165 (1960), 27.

[32]Anthony M. Pasquariello, "Alfonso Sastre: Dramatist with a Mission", Escuadra hacia la muerte, (New York: Appleton--Century--Crofts, 1967), p.1.

[33]"Se trata de Alfonso Sastre....." p. 13.

[34]Jacqueline Chantraine de Van Praag, "Alfonso Sastre: la esperanza del joven teatro español", La Torre, Año 10, 40 (oct.-dic., 1962), 119.

CHAPTER II

SASTRE'S VIEW OF SOCIETY AND DRAMA

As stated in the previous chapter, <u>Drama</u> <u>y</u> <u>socie-</u>
dad represents Sastre's theories concerning drama and
its relationship to and effect on, society. Sastre
professes a distinct social awareness of drama which
for him is synonymous with tragedy or theatre. About
1950 Sastre became aware of the social potential in
the theatre and a majority of his works reveal this
social consciousness. As far as Sastre is concerned,
tragedy is something which functions in society; it is
something contaminated. . . .it favors or obstructs
society from being developed or revolutionized. A
dramatist always writes for his contemporaries in order
to torture them, make them better or to amuse them.
Throughout history, drama has fulfilled diverse functions from the social point of view.[1]

Sastre sees all theatre as a social art. This
includes the most purely artistic theatre. It is a
social art because of its projection on the public,
through its theme and its purpose. Thus, when one
speaks of "social theatre" one expects to find a theatre
characterized by: 1) its projection for large groups
of spectators, 2) its themes, which appeal to masses
of people, and 3) its purpose which reflects the deli-
berate intent of the dramatist to create a socially
purifying experience. The ultimate effect would be a
theatre of propaganda, a political theatre which is
often attained at the expense of the objective purity
of the drama.[2] Thus, there are dramatic forms which
are specifically and strictly social, and they constitute "social theatre". A theatrical performance may
in itself be a social event. From this perspective
one can speak of an "antisocial" theatre, directed
towards the proletariat, with the purpose of having a
segregrated class group as an audience. It seems then
that "social" signifies conservative and "antisocial"
connotes revolutionary. Sastre asserts that for a
communist, the theatre considered antisocial by conser-
vatives is the true social theatre.[3] Such theatre is
not intended to provoke disorder but rather to create
a new order. Agreeing with these theories propounded
by Sastre, Ricardo Domenech points out[4] that every
drama acts on society in some form or other. It may
correct , praise or excite the spectator. Thus, drama
in itself is an active reality. It leaves an imprint

on every spectator's conscience and there is an undeniable catharsis. When Domenech utilizes the term "social drama" he means a drama which bases its problems on the problems existent and inherent in that society to which it belongs. The roots of this drama are man and his environs. It must examine the hidden social causes and it is quite possible that this examination will end in a seemingly insoluble question. In trying to comprehend this drama it should be pointed out that Sastre expects theatre to denounce social injustice but without acquiring the dimensions of destructive proletarian propaganda. As indicated, Sastre is irritated by the confusion which often occurs between the terms "social" and "proletarian".[5] A theatre that is purely propaganda (i.e. which reflects a specific ideological stance) is to be abhorred. The duty of the dramatist is to raise certain social, ethical or political questions without being partisan.[6] The dramatist ought to keep his personal ideology a mystery. He should permit his characters to voice their beliefs without injecting a personal note into the opinion. One therefore must seek the playwright's ideas in other works and not in his purely dramatic works. He must give voice to his characters as the situation dictates. The dramatist's compromise ends here.[7] Sastre's view is in contrast to that of Camus who believed that any dramatist or novelist injects his own opinion the moment that he elects to treat a particular situation. Sastre therefore, has written numerous essays, published in books and journals, in which he attempts to expose his dramatic theories.[8]

Sastre has been criticized for writing a theatre whose social message appeals to a select minority and not to the theatrical majority; for relaying messages whose meanings are ambiguous; for writing a theatre which at the beginning may seem to signify one thing and in the denouement another. This critic goes so far as to state that at times one needs the shrewdness of a detective in order to decipher the social intent of the playwright. He cites three specific examples of this as follows: Muerte en el barrio, El pan de todos and La cornada.[9] It must be argued however, that this is a rather harsh accusation since the social intent of the dramatist is clear. Perhaps what confuses the issue is that no solution to the dilemma is offered. The spectator, if he is to conform with Sastre's intent, must provide his own answers to the problem. Sastre has acknowledged that he does not present

16

any solutions but defends his position by declaring that art is not supposed to indicate any solution for the conflicts which are presented.[10] Sastre has further countered that the artistically poor play is always socially bad. Yet the artistically good can be socially bad. He affirms that the popularity of a work is not a social or artistic criterion. Thus, Sastre says that he never identified the "social theatre" with the "popular theatre". Unpopularity, however, he sees as a negative criterion. On this question of popularity, another critic[11] has accused Sastre of expecting the public to turn to him and abandon the cinema merely because the content of his work is social; however, he adds, the language of the cinema is more suited to the psychology of the masses than is the theatre. For this reason, the masses will never turn to the theatre.

When Sastre utilizes the word "tragedy" it signifies something more than the usual connotation. When tragedy ends, the spectator's spirit has been purified; the effect on the spectator is immediate, and consequently there is a later indirect effect on society. Tragedy becomes a social virtue.[12] Sastre sees drama as the conductive wire through which grief and anguish go from social reality to the heart of the spectator. Through tragedy, the spectator communicates with the anguish of others. Drama is thus converted into the conductive wire between the grief of the street and the spirit of man. Tragedy, he reiterates, is an artistic mechanism which tortures the spectator and leaves him gravely wounded. It is a kind of social sin.[13] In Sastre's definition of tragedy there stands out "an existentialist conception of tragedy; a vision of its agitating quality; a belief in its social effectiveness and an adherence to Aristotelian concepts and terminology".[14]

Sastre has repeatedly used the term social-realismo with respect to his dramas. This term is derived because: 1) Sastre sees art as a true representation of reality and 2) among the different provinces of reality he considers the social problem to be urgent.[15] Other points in this manifesto, which bear relation to this concept, are, the revelation which art makes of reality as a socially progressive element; the judicial function which art fulfills and which makes the artist feel useful to his community--although the latter may reject him at times. Membership in a political movement does not signify the loss of autonomy for the artist. In fact, this compromise is the expression of his liberty.

17

On the other hand, non-membership in a political movement does not mean that the artist is inhibited or that
he is betraying the social responsibility which is de-
manded in his work. The principal function of art in
this unjust world is to transform it and the "urgency"
of that art is the stimulus to transform the existing
social order. Only a work of great aesthetic quality
is capable of transforming the world. This art of
urgency is what Sastre terms social-realismo. Sastre
does not see social-realismo as a formula for art and
literature. Social-realismo functions in the artist's
supposed quality of independence or liberty. Another
supposed factor is the superaction of the liberal conception of art, according to which, art is a supreme
category. This term for Sastre immediately connotes
1) the category of the theme 2) the nature of the intention of the artist, and 3) the mode of artistic
treatment.[16] This in turn means that the theme is to
be social in nature, that the artist is to be aware
that his work may have degenerative or revolutionary
repercussions and that realism is to be the artistic
form utilized in order to provoke the required agitation
on the part of the spectator. Sastre concludes by pointing out that the aesthetic emotion provoked by the
social-realistic literature results in the legacy of a
permanent nucleus which is projected in a socially purifying manner.

Sastre's social-realism is evident in the plays
which Farris Anderson has categorized as the dramas of
social-realism and which are "based on the pressures
which certain situations or a general human condition
bring to bear on human beings and they offer no con-
clusive answers or solutions".[17] These plays comply
with the dramatist's principles in presenting characters who are existential creatures and also men of
action. These characters are never super-beings but
rather creatures who suffer the anguish of having to
endure a particular situation from which they can only
escape if certain conditions are modified. Thus, success often results in tragic consequences.

The pursuit of social-realism in Sastre's plays is
reflected both in the action and in the settings which
make social injustice very apparent. Even though the
geographical setting is not always clearly established,
the social purport is unquestionable. Sastre deals with
characters who are revolutionary activists, with a
society and family dominated by tyranny, with a working-

class barrio and with the socially exploited individual
--all of which represent a social-realistic background.
The dramatic situation contained within this background
revolves around the individual who is required to exe-
cute a particular act, the consequences of which will
have a personally disastrous effect on said individual.
As it has been pointed out, Sastre is concerned "with
the results of individual action in society... [conse-
quently] his drama is oriented toward an improved social
state". [18]

Sastre postulates that on many occasions the theatre
has served the revolution.[19] He explains this by asser-
ting that the revolutionary act is the source of political theatre. Social anguish resounds on the stage.
Through the voice of the dramatist, revolutionary groups
express their hope in new forms. The playwright sees
two faces of the political theatre: 1) that which denounces misery and horror and 2) that which advocates
hope in new social structures. Therefore, authors of
the revolution justify the shedding of blood on account
of that misery, and at the same time declare their hope
in the changes which are to come. Sastre again denotes
the dangers of falling into the purely propagandistic
path in which the antagonist is converted into a monster and the protagonist into a saintly hero. Consequently, the engagement has to be founded on an objective vision of social-political reality. In order to
further emphasize this point Sastre states that the
reason for the failure of Jean-Paul Sartre's Le Diable
et le bon Dieu lies primarily in the fact that Sartre
sacrificed everything to ideology. Sastre adds further
that the dramatist can lead the audience to the truth
if he permits the drama to function on its own plane
and only expresses his ideas in parentheses.[20] In this
way he may be the first to be astonished at the ideology
of the play.

According to Sastre dogmatism merely serves to
stifle the objective purity of drama. Sastre believes
in being committed to the struggle for social change
yet he hesitates at revealing any distinct ideology.
This appears to be one area of self-contradiction for
which Sastre has been criticized. The placing of these
limits on the dramatist is paradoxical since the author
clearly sees a revolutionary theatre as a companion
development to both the Russian and Mexican Revolutions.
Obviously these theatres professed a specific ideology.
In Sastre's contradiction, the ideological commitment

on the one hand, and the purpose of agitation on the other, the latter clearly emerges as the more espoused element. Thus, from the many demands that Sastre makes with respect to the theatre, the one which stands out is the element of agitation. This becomes more apparent after one takes into consideration the undermining of the aesthetic to the moral and social, the rejection of a propagandist literature and the postulation of a social-realist theatre synonymous with a socially purifying realistic theatre.

It has been suggested that Sastre's theatre is "revolutionary" in more than one sense, since "everyone of Sastre's plays betrays a profound preoccupation with man's problems and the meaning of his existence... [and] they represent a revolt against the provincialism of the Spanish Theatre".[21] Sastre's desire to agitate the spectator is borne out by a critic who declares that the "spectator is moved by a drama of Galdós, is amazed with one of Lorca but is agitated with one of Sastre".[22] By means of this agitation Sastre expects social injustice to be corrected but the method which he employs is that of criminal investigation--apparent particularly in Muerte en el barrio, Asalto nocturno, and La mordaza but less obvious in a majority of others. There are specific examples of revolutionary theatre as evidenced in Prólogo patético, Escuadra hacia la muerte, Tierra roja, En la red and Guillermo Tell tiene los ojos tristes. In fact this trend of thought continues throughout Sastre's theatre with a few exceptions which could be termed the asocial plays--namely Ana Kleiber, El cuervo and La sangre de Dios, as well as the four early plays of the Arte Nuevo group. The themes of these plays are distinctly asocial and deal specifically with non-related issues.

With respect to the thematic content of a play, Sastre affirms that although all theatrical themes are social, one can still speak of a "social theme".[23] These occur when there are themes of "dramatic reality" in which large human groups are interested. However, this does not mean that society rather than an individual becomes the protagonist. The dramatist intends that the drama which has been extracted from reality should reflect reality. The social extraction which he has effected should resound in society and serve as its purification. Sastre questions the basis for the social injustice which has been inflicted and since injustice usually implies some criminal or guilty party,

the criminal investigation is the means of ascertaining
where the origin of guilt lies. At times this question
is but a rhetorical one, as in Escuadra hacia la muerte,
and very often it is the unifying element in Sastre's
varied dramatic output. Bacause of this investigative
nature inherent in Sastre's theatre, the theme of guilt
is a recurrent one. Together with the theme of guilt
one can detect those of social injustice, human anxiety,
war, terror and fear; fate, social and personal rebellion; solitude, love and disillusionment, time, religious fervor and uncertainty and death. Love is perhaps
the only one which is significantly non-recurring. Because of the reappearance of these themes, Sastre's
theatre has often been characterized as pessimistic in
its outlook on man and contemporary society. However,
a careful, more detailed analysis of all his plays
would indicate that this does not reflect Sastre's total
outlook. There is a frequency of death and suffering
in Sastre's plays but very often the questions raised
in the denouement lead one to conclude that the dramatist
sees some other alternative to the existing condition
and that it is up to man to exercise his prerogative in
order to terminate the socially unjust conditions under
which he has been living. It must be emphasized, however, that frequently this is attained only after one
endures great personal sacrifice.

Investigation concerning guilt and responsibility,[24]
takes place on both the social and metaphysical planes.
The question of man's suffering and death is by no means
novel and Sastre, without providing any answers whatso-
ever, raises the question of original sin and death as
perpetrating an eternal punishment. The question raised
on the metaphysical level produces an agonizing catharsis
in the spectator whose fear and pity are aroused through
a feeling of personal guilt. "Sastre measures the degree of catharsis--and thus the effectiveness of a given
tragedy--by the impact of the spectator's purgation on
the reality of his circumstances.."[25] Although Sastre
is more concerned with the social injustices that exist
than with the personal anguish suffered by his protagonists, he nevertheless, uses the latter as the initia-
ting factor of each play. He acknowledges that the individual is an anguished being with respect to death
but he reaffirms the importance of the collective aspect
of the individual situation.

Examining the dramas of social-realism it becomes
clear that revolution becomes the "thematic axle".[26]

In these dramas, the characters are men and women who are thrown together in the struggle for an improved society. Some act collectively as in _Tierra roja_ and _Muerte en el barrio_, while others such as Tell in _Guillermo Tell tiene los ojos tristes_ and Luisa of _La mordaza_ are forced to initiate the action and thus suffer personal grief or anguish. Because of strong revolutionary intent, Sastre has not created powerful individualistic types, excepting perhaps Tell, but this does not detract from the effectiveness of the drama since the author's intent is clearly visible. For a clear understanding of what Sastre means by social-realism it is essential to examine the dramas of social-realism in detail. The first group that can be defined is perhaps that of revolution. Among these are _Escuadra hacia la muerte_ which deals with war; _Prólogo patético_, _En la red_, _El pan de todos_, _Tierra roja_ and _Guillermo Tell tiene los ojos tristes_ which deal with political revolution; and _Muerte en el barrio_ and _La mordaza_ which deal with social and personal problems and are indirectly related to this theme of revolution.

When _Escuadra hacia la muerte_ was first performed in 1953, there was a distinct impression which remained with the public. As Pérez Minik has pointed out, there were three distinct effects produced: "Primero, porque hasta este momento, después de nuestra guerra, no se había llevado al escenario un episodio bélico donde el valor y la significación de la lucha por las armas entre los hombres se sometiera a debates polémicos. Segundo, porque la interpretación que de esta guerra y de estos personajes podía entresacarse en parte, era clara y en parte oscura, y tercero, porque teníamos ante nuestros ojos, también como excepcional ocasión, un drama social de acción directa, terminante y contundente, expuesto en una forma desconocida en nuestro país, densa y sustantiva."[27] Consequently, the death of Goban put an end to the abuse of power, a reign of tyranny and the unjust state of affairs but did not resolve anything. In this play, five soldiers and their corporal Goban constitute a condemned squad in the Third World War. Their orders are to form the vanguard for their own troops and to lie in wait for the enemy. Their only mission is to blow up a mine field and die. Thus, there is to be no way out for these men. They have enough provisions to last two months. The men resent Goban's authoritarian and cruel manner and after having imbibed quantities of alcohol they attack and kill the corporal. This action takes place in part I. In part II they bury

the corporal and are prepared to wait out their time
undisciplined, unwashed and ill-prepared. Pedro seemingly takes over as leader and urges them to turn
themselves in, since, with the exception of Luis who
was on guard duty when Goban was murdered, they are
all guilty. Finally, each decides to go his own way.
Pedro intends to turn himself in, Javier commits suicide, Andrés and Adolfo go off in the woods and then
separate. Andrés, exhausted, decides to await the
enemy while Adolfo goes off and is presumably lost in
the forest. Luis, the only one who will survive, is
to be "cursed with living". He offers to admit his
guilt even though he did not take part in the crime.
Death would be preferable to him than having to live
alone. Pedro suggests that this will perhaps be Luis'
eternal punishment.

Within this play the anguish of the unknown, the
fear of death and solitude and the lack of human togetherness are dominant. Herein Sastre presents a
drama devoid of any ideology even though some critics
have erroneously suggested that this is purely anti-
war in sentiment. It is much more than that. The
antimilitaristic note is echoed in the unsympathetic
presentation of Corporal Goban and in his harsh, unrea-
listic values of life. Goban is utterly cruel, completely lacking in sentiment and the reason he is one
of the condemned squad is because he killed three of
his own men. Luis' only sin is that he refused to join
a firing squad. Pedro's sin is killing prisoners of
war in cold blood in order to avenge the rape of his
wife by enemy soldiers. Javier, the philosopher, was
a coward in that he refused to kill and commit other
acts of violence. Andrés had abandoned his parents
and mistress because of purely selfish reasons and had
killed a sergeant while in an alcoholic stupor. Adolfo
was involved in a blackmarket deal with community bread
(a theme which is fully developed in El pan de todos)
and informed on one of his allies. He is utterly un-
repentant for his past actions. He is the one who
initiates the act of killing Goban. After the death of
Goban, the lack of any military discipline makes worth-
less slobs of these men who are completely without purpose or direction. This counteracts the idea that the
play is purely antimilitaristic. While Goban lived,
there was a sense of purpose for the condemned men.
With Goban's death, anarchy sets in and the sense of
purpose disappears. All these characters are essentially tragic and tormented creatures. They sinned against

society by taking justice into their own hands. Now
they must suffer the consequences. Although Luis will
live, his sentence amounts to a "life sentence" within
society. As one critic has indicated, the real theme
is what Eugene O'Neill called "not the relation of man
to man but the relation of man to God. It is the dilemma of living and dying found in plays of O'Neill, Sartre,
Beckett..."[28]

The question of original sin is raised by Javier,
who declares that Goban's death was part of a master
plan to punish them:

> Estamos marcados, Pedro. Estamos
> marcados. Rezar, ¿para qué? ¿a
> quién? Rezar....Sí. Hay alguien
> que nos castiga por algo..., por
> algo... Debe haber..., sí, a fin
> de cuentas, habrá que creer en
> eso... Una falta...de origen...
> Un misterioso y horrible pecado...
> del que no tenemos ni idea. Puede
> que haga mucho tiempo."[29]

The fear of death and of the unknown torture these men.
They cannot be saved now because Goban was the one who
was to show them the way to salvation. "Necesito una
escuadra de soldados para la muerte. Los tendré. Los
haré de vosotros... Voy a morir con vosotros. Pero vais
a la muerte limpios, en perfecto estado de revista" (172).
Since they have destroyed the only possible way to salvation, they must now flounder in "confusion, bewilder-
ment, enigma and remorse".[30] It is interesting to note
how each man reacts now that their official leader is
out of the way. At first it seemed like an act of self-
liberation but as time goes by they realize that their
only means of exit has been cut off. According to one
critic Goban's death affects the men in two ways. "Su
presencia, su actitud y sus exigencias habían dado un
sentido al hacer del grupo y proporcionaba el factor de
unión. Su muerte elimina el elemento aglutinante y
posibilita el desbande. De aquí viene la mayor diferen-
cia de la primera y la segunda parte. En ésta los soldados son hombres relativamente libres que, como tales,
deben dar sus propias respuestas y tomar sus propias
decisiones."[31] Pedro tries to resume leadership telling
the others that they should continue as before and try
to fulfill their mission. In addition they should confess how Goban died. Adolfo rejects this last idea

thinking that they may be able to extricate themselves
from their present position and continue to live. Pedro,
however, replies, "A mí me parece que hay cosas más
importantes que vivir. Me daría mucha vergüenza seguir
viviendo. Ya no podría ser feliz nunca." (209) Pedro
of course has his personal reasons for not wanting to
live, consequently this statement of his does not necessarily mean that his willingness to sacrifice himself
is solely on account of Goban's death. Death to Pedro
is preferable to a few miserable years more of life.
He sees the sacrifice perhaps as a means of expurgation
while Adolfo on the other hand sees no need for this
and views life as an entity in itself. As we see here
the social themes of guilt and responsibility are in-
tertwined. The responsibility for their actions and
even for their own lives frightens these men. Goban
and later Pedro are the only ones who are ready to face
the consequences. Seen in this light, Goban is not a
completely negative personality and bears out the thesis
that Sastre's antiheroes are not complete monsters.
Luis, the one who has no positive stain on his character,
is so weak that he looks fearfully toward his future
existence. Pedro who presumably might be identified as
the hero, if indeed there is one, did participate in
Goban's death and was guilty of mass murder. Again, we
have no saint. Nevertheless, Van der Naald sees Pedro
as the author's mouthpiece for his belief in shouldering
one's responsibility.[32] Van der Naald adds that Goban,
Adolfo and Pedro reflect the apparent paradox between
antimilitarism and praise of military discipline, but
she sees this dissolved by Pedro who recognizes the need
for an inner discipline in man rather than the exterior
one imposed by another man. Another interesting point
made by this critic is that Adolfo turns out to be the
most disagreeable of the characters since Goban, cruel
and harsh though he was, believed in ideals though they
were false. In this play Sastre presents a situation
which has tragic overtones in spite of the fact that
some of these characters did commit crimes. Yet social
injustice is evident in the person of Luis, whose only
crime was to refuse to be a member of a firing squad.
After the problems that so many American youths have
had to face for refusing to take part in the Vietnam
War, we cannot but accept the social realism inherent
in Sastre's play. The message that Sastre intends is
concrete. He remains faithful to his principle in this
respect. Nine years after the performance of this play,
Sastre wrote in a prologue to the Obras Completas that
this play was intended as a shout of protest in the face

25

of the threat of a new world war. He clarifies this
adding that it is "una negación de la validez de las
grandes palabras con que en las guerras se camufla el
horror; una negación en ese sentido, del heroísmo y de
toda mística de la muerte. La muerte no es hermosa...
Mi obra es también un examen de conciencia, o mejor
dicho, una invitación al examen de conciencia de una
generación de dirigentes que parecía dispuesta, en el
silencioso clamor de la guerra fría, a conducirnos
al matadero". (161-162). It is clear then, that this
is a loud anti-war cry. Sastre adds further that if he
were to rewrite Escuadra hacia la muerte, that he would
in addition affirm the beauty and necessity of peace.

Prólogo patético is the first of Sastre's plays
which deals with social revolution. In keeping with
the idea of a prologue, this theme is not fully developed as it is in some of the the later works. Beneath
the acts of terrorism which are part of any revolution
lies the moral conflict which torments the character
Oscar. This conflict between the social issue on the
one hand and the moral, here allied to the familial, is
apparent in all of these dramas of revolution and personal rebellion. Here Sastre presents a number of men
who are all young terrorists. Oscar has been selected
to throw a bomb at an appointed time and place. He is
willing to fight for the cause but is tormented by the
shedding of innocent blood. He gladly suffers imprisonment and torture in the name of the revolution. However, he is led by the police to believe falsely that
his brother Julio perished in the bomb blast and this
adds to Oscar's torment. The idea of a family having
been sacrificed for the cause, fills Oscar with much
anguish. In the meantime, believing the story of the
police Oscar, justifiably angry, kills Pablo, a fellow
terrorist, whom he blames for his own actions. After
he realizes that Julio is alive, and that he was tricked
by the police, he laments the uselessness of Pablo's
death. He did it merely because of a theoretical justification. Oscar's torment now is that he is useless.
He decides that what matters now is to suffer for the
cause. "Seré útil a la causa sufriendo..., aguantando
las torturas en aquel sótano inmundo hasta que digan:
'Es inútil. Este partido es invencible. Sus hombres
se dejan matar sin mover los labios'" (105). Thus he
complacently awaits the arrival of the Police and looks
forward to being taken away. The moral issue here is,
revolutionary violence.

Another young terrorist, Antón, is tormented at the

thought of killing nameless people. (66-68). He is no
anarchist yet feels that perhaps these acts of terrorism are justified in the name of social justice. Sastre's presentation here is one of inner perplexity in
the face of such a question--Can these acts of terrorism be justified? How can they achieve social justice? Farris Anderson points out that this is not
"merely an abstract moral conflict, for Oscar it at-
tains existential significance: in order to justify
one's existence it is necessary to justify one's acts,
and Oscar is not at all convinced that his acts are
justified. Thus Sastre again achieves a merger of existential and social crises."[33] Oscar declares that if
the revolution succeeds, then the death of innocent victims was essential. Julio, however, counteracts this
by saying that if men truly loved one another, then the
revolution would not be necessary. The unexpressed
thought, however, is that men do not love one another,
so this is why there are revolutions. The moral ambiguity here offers no rapid solution. Sastre hesitates
at offering a definite ideological answer. As Anderson
puts it, later on Sastre's "question is no longer whether revolution is morally justified, but simply how
it is to be carried out".[34] The implication being that
one can justify revolutionary tactics under certain
given conditions yet, given these circumstances, the
conflict be it moral or familial continues to haunt one.
El cubo de la basura contains elements which can be con-
trasted with those of Prólogo patético. In this play
the protagonist Germán is an anarchist who takes the
matter of justice into his own hands. He is not concerned like the other characters with the collective
rectification of social injustice. Consequently, social
revolution is of no interest to him. Here the personal
issue takes precedence over the social. Sastre himself
declares that "el autor del crimen no es más que un
anarquista, producido por nuestro tiempo, indiferente
a los movimientos colectivos, incrédulo de la justicia
social (y, coherentemente, de la llamada injusticia
social); un hombre que cree, sin rodeos, que uno tiene
que tomarse la justicia por su mano. La actitud del
invisible antagonista no provoca en él angustias de
orden social y antagonismos colectivos, de clase a
clase. Estamos ante un antimarxista puro." (109).

In this play some of the violence related to the
revolution has already occurred. More is yet to come--
thus the revolution is by no means over. Germán's
father died for the cause; yet Germán tells Señor Tomás,

27

the father of his friend Julia, that he still goes hungry while those involved in the worker's struggle live as they please. For this reason he has no interest in politics. What does interest Germán is Julia. He was in love with her but she ran off from the barrio with a lover who later abandoned her when he found out that she had tuberculosis. She has now returned to her parents' home. Germán then leaves the barrio and seeks out Julia's former lover Pablo and kills him for having abandoned Julia. Germán kills for purely personal reasons. In spite of Germán's disinterest in the cause the political activists meet at his mother's home. A minor character Luis also declares his unwillingness to take part. He has endured enough suffering and for what purpose? He declares, "No hay nada que hacer. Conmigo, por lo menos, que no cuenten. Yo he luchado y ya tengo bastante. Al final tuve la mala pata de que me hicieran los de la C.N.T. y este pulmón no estará ya bueno nunca. Se perdió la guerra y además murió la mujer. No tuve ya nada. Ahora ¿dónde estoy? Aquí, en el cubo de la basura. Donde tengo que estar. Nunca debí salir de este asqueroso sitio. Parece que cada uno tiene su lugar en este mundo y que es idiota buscar otra cosa. El que nace para pudrirse, se pudre..." (132-133). The fatalistic attitude that was apparent in Escuadra hacia la muerte reappears here. The "coronel" who appears in order to incite the workers once more to the cause, rejects Luis' arguments and urges him to have more stamina. While the activists are holding a meeting in Germán's home, the Police arrive to arrest him for the murder of Pablo. It is interesting to see how Germán rationalizes his killing of Pablo. As far as he is concerned, he committed no crime. "He matado a un hombre..., pero era un hombre que estaba fuera de la ley, o por lo menos, de mi ley ....Ese no era honrado y se había portado cruelmente con alguien. Estaba al margen de la ley, y le he castigado" (151). This play is one of the least effective of Sastre's collection. A critic blames its fragmented structure on the lack of thematic unity which exists because of the separateness of the individual's personal problem and the social protest. At the same time this same critic declares that "La mayor debilidad de la obra consiste en que no ofrece una relación definitiva entre por un lado, la probreza y la sublevación proyectada, y por otro, el crimen de Germán."[35] It should be pointed out here that this play has never been performed, perhaps because of its slight dramatic value and the weak delineation of the characters. In addition, because the social issue has been obscured by the personal, Sastre has failed to pursue his own dialectic principles which at this time, however, were not yet fully developed.

In _Tierra roja_ the collective social issue is fully treated. This play also has never been performed in spite of its extraordinary documentary value concerning the life of Spanish miners.[36] Unlike _El cubo de la basura_, the revolutionary atmosphere is indisputable. This play has a cyclical character with no beginning and no end. It is reminiscent of Lope de Vega's _Fuenteovejuna_ in the collective admission of guilt which the interrogators receive from the miners. The plot unfolds with the imminent departure of Pedro and his family from the company house which they had occupied throughout Pedro's service in the mines. The custom is that, on retiring, the worker has to vacate the premises and seek shelter outside the mining company's territory. A young miner, Pablo, has just arrived in town and is shocked by this social injustice. Enraged, he organizes some fellow workers to resist this company practice by striking. At Pablo's insistence the workers convene outside Pedro's house at his scheduled hour of departure and Pedro, his wife Teresa, and daughter Inés, are urged to remain inside. Pedro, who is reluctant to carry through with Pablo's plan, warns Pablo that the only result will be bloodshed. The workers resist the attempt of the police to disperse them and there is bloodshed on both sides. Innocent victims are among the dead. A baby is killed in the _melée_. This incident causes an upsurge of anger which is a feature later developed in _Muerte en el barrio_.

In the epilogue it is learned that Inés lost both her parents in the revolt of the miners. She is now married to Pablo and it is now their turn to vacate their home. A young man arrives just as Pablo had done years previously and talks with them and their daughter. It is through the "Joven" that Pablo realizes that all is not the same and that all the suffering has not been in vain. As Inés enters the room, Pablo shouts to her that on the following day they will refuse to leave. Just as Pedro had acquiesced to Pablo's demands because he felt that he was doing something to improve everyone's lot, so Pablo feels that his refusal to leave is being done on the behalf of others. The implication here is that the resistance will have some effect because it is going to be organized and well controlled rather than

just a sporadic attempt at insurrection. The irony of
the situation is that although the lot of the miner is
a bleak one, nevertheless, it is preferable to the
situation which awaits an unemployed man in the city.
When Pablo first arrived in the mining town he had
declared that he would not remain there all his life.
This is exactly how Pedro had felt years before.
Although work in the mines is hell to them they are not
equiped to handle anything else. Inés is the one who
reflects the men's attitude: "... Mi padre cuenta que
la primera vez que bajó a la mina, a los dieciocho años,
le pareció que había entrado en el infierno..., y ahora
que ya no va a poder bajar está triste..." (353). The
feeling that one has outlived his usefulness is too
much to bear. Both Pedro and Pablo had to overcome
their fears as older men before capitulating to the
insistence of the young men. The feeling of inevitabi-
lity was strong yet they were both able to overcome
these feelings in the face of collective action. One
gets the impression that Sastre believes in collective
rebellion. A solitary act achieves nothing but failure
and suffering; but a united act carries some hope with
it.

Guillermo Tell tiene los ojos tristes represents
the opposite situation to Tierra roja. Here, a solitary
individual is forced by certain circumstances to take
matters into his own hands. It is after his initial
action which brings him much grief and pain that the
people show any serious signs of unity. It is this
aspect of the Tell myth which Sastre chooses to emphasize. "Tell deja de ser el protagonista de una proeza
para convertirse en el sujeto de una tragedia. Adquiere,
en ese tratamiento, la grandeza de un redentor por cuyo
sacrificio es posible la salvación de los otros. Es
destruido para que vivan los demás. En su corazón no
habrá ya nunca alegría, pero su pueblo será feliz" (587).
Here is a country ruled by the tyrannical governor
Gessler. No one dares to disobey him. Regardless of
social strata, Gessler is hated by everyone. According
to one source, "Gessler expresa el orden, la tranquili-
dad, la inmovilidad..[Tell] no es un revolucionario de
un partido, de una organización, de una asamblea.
Alfonso Sastre ataca en su obra los métodos de la demo-
cracia... Asimismo ataca la disciplina, los procedimi-
entos discursivos, el funcionarismo. Guillermo Tell
expresa el acto creador puro, en esta circunstancia, el
acto revolucionario puro, anárquico, personal, el in-
transferible, no sabemos si decir el providencial."[37]

Sastre's plot differs from the well known myth in that when Tell is ordered by the governor to shoot an arrow through an apple placed on his son's head, Tell misses his target and kills his son. In his grief and outrage he kills the governor and his country is liberated from its tyrant. Tell does commit the revolutionary act but this is almost accidental for he is not by character revolutionary. He does what he must for personal reasons which are all family-oriented. His act has nothing to do with the retribution of wrongs committed toward others. This dreamy, romantic figure is converted into a man of action who acts only because he cannot stand the personal grief and indignity to which he has been subjected. Tell's emotions are profoundly human yet at the same time he is an unwilling anarchist.

Is Sastre condoning anarchy? The answer has to be negative when we see Tell in all his pain and loneliness. It has been suggested that Tell's slight exposure to the public is not sufficient to arouse the audience's empathy.[38] This assumption must be refuted, for Tell's suffering after the act is moving and converts him into a sympathetic tragic figure. Sastre presents Tell, after his son's death, with deep sensitivity. What Sastre achieves with this play is a parody of dictatorship as well as the burden to be borne by the reluctant victim responsible for the destruction of tyrannical order. There are many serious questions posed by Sastre in this play concerning religious conviction, social injustice, familial bonds and personal faith in Man as well as God.

With respect to En la red, Sastre has said that this is a drama "sobre la condición humana del 'hombre clandestino'" (795). For this reason it has been suggested that this drama, "a pesar de su contenido teóricamente exótico, no es sino un profundo y tenso alegato, en nombre de la dignidad humana, contra la injusticia, crueldad y opresión."[39] Although the action takes place in Algeria, this drama could be situated in any country with a totalitarian regime. This play has been classified as an example of what constitutes pure dramatic literature for it is a "teatro despojado de adornos inútiles."[40] According to the playwright himself "es el fin último del teatro concebido como forma de lucha y de investigación de lo real."[41] This statement is borne out by the plot and structure in which political activists are hiding in an abandoned building while the police dragnet which has been thrown over the city, draws nearer. The realism achieved here reflects the torture and solitary existence which the clandestine man is forced to endure if he expects the existing regime to be finally overthrown.

Pablo and Celia, two of the clandestine activists who are already in the apartment, are later joined by Leo, the latter's husband who has just escaped from the police after suffering police brutality. The suspicion and mistrust which is part of the daily life of the pursued is evident in Celia's and Leo's attitude to Pablo, whom they suspect of being a police spy. Celia wants to believe in Pablo but cannot. She admits to Pablo her fears concerning him since he could very well be "un policía que espera a que este refugio le revele sus secretos. Un policía que se ha metido en la red y que en cualquier momento puede ordenar: '¡Arriba! ¡Ya es bastante!'" (812). What makes the situation even more difficult is that Pablo admits that he cannot show her any proof of his identity. As Celia and Pablo fear, the police net finally reaches them. Leo is shot as he runs out onto the balcony and Celia and Pablo are taken away.

There are two noteworthy aspects of the denouement. The first is the way in which Hanafi (another member of the clandestine group) includes the audience in his bitter pronouncement "Asesinos". (862). The implication is that the spectator is to be blamed for the social injustice which he has just witnessed. Sastre blames us all for the crime and the humiliation of man's dignity. Secondly, the apparent positive attitude which Pablo and Celia present leads one to hope in the success of the revolution if they are able to withstand the torture. There is a hint of victory but it will be at considerable expense—both physical and emotional. This particular glimpse of victory is indeed ambiguous and the spectator cannot be absolutely sure whether there is total triumph for the activists or total annihilation of them. Sastre has been criticized for being partial to the rebels and for showing the cruelties of one side only. Sastre of course expected such reactions and as he says in the "Autocrítica", he is concerned with showing an aspect of reality which should touch the conscience of the spectator. What Sastre achieves conforms to his dialectical principles—arousal of anguish in the spectator but with a tinge of hope at the end.

In El pan de todos, the revolution has already been

32

realized--at least its violent aspect. The actual rebellion has already taken place and what remains now
is to see just how well this revolution functions. Thus
the country is still in a revolutionary phase. This
play was considered subversive and was denied performance in 1954. Yet, in 1957 it was considered anti-
revolutionary and its performance was authorized. Here
then is the classic example of the ambiguities which
exist in much of Sastre's theatre. In the "noticia"
to this play Sastre declares that he sees revolution as
a tragic reality. With respect to the tone of his dramas, he affirms that "queda claro en ellos que si toda
revolución es un hecho trágico, todo orden social in-
justo es una tragedia sorda inaceptable" (226). He
adds further that he is deliberately placing the spectator in the dilemma of having to choose between the
two tragedies. It seems evident to him that the tragedy of unjust social order can only be destroyed by
revolutionary tragedy. Thus, the revolution is always
a tragic entity.

This play which takes place in a communist country,
begins with a party meeting at which David Harko, the
protagonist, urges a purification to cleanse the party
of traitors who are informing against them. Most of
this drama is concerned with the moral dilemma in which
David finds himself when he is informed that his mother
has been guilty of placing her personal interests above
those of the common welfare. She has been guilty of
taking money from Pedro Yudd, a profiteer, because she
believes that the revolution has failed and she wants
to leave the country with her son David and his wife.
David becomes depressed at the realization that the
conditions of the peasants and workers are worse than
before. "Las cosas van peor de lo que yo creía. En
muchos sitios la situación de los obreros y campesinos
es más terrible, más cruel que antes de la Revolución.
Estamos siendo traicionados..." (244). Because of this
he and others have asked the Central Committee for an
order to purge the party of profiteers. The persistent
hunger of the people worries David. He is totally committed to the revolution. He tells his wife Marta that
it is surprising how many old and beloved friends are
guilty of betrayal. Yet he is firm in his conviction
that the order be severe so that an example be set.
When Yudd is accused of making deals with the people's
bread he compromises David's mother Juana. David, in
his blind faithfulness to the party and its cause, refuses to try to extricate his mother from the political

33

web and she is executed. Subsequently, David cannot live with himself and commits suicide.

The ideological ambiguity evidenced in David's torment and suicide is what has caused this play to be attacked from opposing political view points. Sastre here presents a country in which the revolution's aims are being undermined. The struggle between the personal and social order is presented without there being any way out of the dilemma but suicide. The relativity of the social values is what is being questioned. Anderson declares, Sastre "shows that the revolutionary ideal is inevitably subject to contamination by individual egos and that a political system can be established and defended only through a pragmatic distortion of truth."[42] With regard to the reaction of critics, to the ambiguities embodied in El pan de todos, it must be pointed out that various critics have extracted distinct messages from this play. Haro Tecglen sees it as anticommunist; García Pavón says that David was corrupted by society and his aunt Paula. Yet Giuliano sees David as one who is disposed to make the ultimate sacrifice on behalf of the revolution. As Giuliano sees it, "lo que impide la revolución es el egoísmo de la naturaleza humana."[43] A significant factor concerning the end of this play relates to the official announcement of David's death. A senior party official, Jacobo Fessler, orders that David's death be designated as accidental and that "sus últimas palabras fueron de solidaridad para la causa, de amor al Partido y de fe en el porvenir...David Harko es un ejemplo para las juventudes del Partido...David...es un héroe de la Revolución" (278). The bitter irony of this lie is not lost on the spectator. The fact that the Party has to submit to such a lie is evidence of its lost cause. The message clearly is that the revolution is concerned with abstractions, mere philosophical questions and not with human beings—not with the individual in society.

In the "Noticia" to Muerte en el barrio, Sastre declares that he is concerned with the relationship between a sick person and the doctor and even more so with the social organization of medicine. Sastre is also concerned with the frequent lack of vocation among doctors and the common deficiencies of their ethical code. The weaknesses apparent in socialized medicine, particularly the depersonalization of the patient, is also of interest to the playwright. This play has never been performed, apparently because of the fact of the fear of offending doctors.[44] This play presents a situation in which a child who has suffered an accident is taken to a clinic but the doctor who should be on duty is absent and the child dies. The negligence of the doctor results in his murder by an angry group of citizens among whom is the child's father Arturo. This drama portrays an innocent victim amidst an unjust social system--one in which a doctor who is solely interested in research is made to practice medicine because of economic necessity. He neglects his social responsibility. But is he solely responsible for the child's death; or is society, which placed him in a compromising situation, to shoulder the full burden? This is the rhetorical question raised in this drama.

The actual dramatization occurs when a police inspector goes to the tavern in order to investigate the murder of Dr. Sanjo. The crime has been committed by a group and is an indication of collective rebellion. The drama unfolds when the tavern keeper narrates the events as they occurred. It is interesting to note that the inspector seems to be satisfied that the crime was committed by a spontaneous act--one which supposedly is justified. However, Sastre addes atmospheric elements to the supposed justification. The unbearable heat has affected the authors of the crime and it seems that the act was committed under atmospheric pressure. This climatic element is used as a dramatic device in other plays by Sastre and its function therein has been questioned by Torrente Ballester.[45] It should be pointed out, however, that heat is introduced at the very beginning. It was dramatically functional in Lorca's La casa de Bernada Alba. What should be questioned is not its validity as a device but its effectiveness. By using heat it appears that Sastre wishes to avoid laying the blame totally on society. The element of fate reappears in the form of a climatic condition. In La cornada it is the rain, in La mordaza, the heat, in Escuadra hacia la muerte it is the cold. The symbolic nature of these elements serves to reinforce the realistic effect for which the author is striving.

Clearly Sastre expects us to understand the reason for the actions of Arturo and his companions, yet he does not expect us to condone them. Arturo will be punished for his crime as the inspector insinuates. Consequently, Sastre cannot be seen as an advocate of anarchy. He is merely pointing out the unwarranted injustices existent in society and is making a plea for

the correction of these ills. The problem of socialized medi**cine** and the poor is further emphasized through
Luis, the consumptive patient who is practically ostracized by society for the type of illness he has and
also for his financial inability to receive treatment
and hospital services. Luis echoes the plight of the
poor when he says, "¿sabes lo peor que le puede ocurrir
a un hombre pobre, Genoveva? Enfermar. Enfermar, eso
es lo peor que le puede ocurrir en este mundo" (568).
If the child's family had been able to afford it, they
too could have availed themselves of the services of a
private practitioner but their economic situation de-
prived them of this. The child was a victim of social
ills.

La mordaza does not deal with social revolution
but rather with a family rebellion. In the play, however, the family is but a symbol of the larger family--
society--and the individual family members react as do
the individual members of society. The tyrannical
father Isaías Krappo is the symbol of an oppressive
ruler. He is to his family, what Gessler (in Guillermo
Tell tiene los ojos tristes) is to his subjects. The
family's fear of Isaías is reflective of one's fear of
a tyrannical ruler. The family is a society in minia-
ture. Performance of this play was authorized without
any problems since society itself is not criticized.
The question of guilt and responsibility is interestingly presented. Isaías commits a crime for which he is
apprehended. He killed in cold blood a man who threatened his life, because Isaías had murdered the man's
wife and daughter during the war. The question, of
whether Isaías is a villain or a hero, is raised when
he tells the police commissioner, "Que si a ese hombre
lo hubiera matado hace cuatro años, tú te hubieras
puesto muy contento. Y que yo, por lo mismo que ahora
soy un criminal, entonces hubiera sido un héroe...¿No
te hace gracia? Uno es un héroe o un criminal según
las circunstancias, aunque el muerto sea el mismo" (335).
The commissioner agrees that Isaías killed at the inop-
portune moment. Society then condemns Isaías for this
crime which, if he had committed it during the war,
would have earned him a hero's acclaim! Such are the
inconsistencies dictated by society. La mordaza represents the gag or silence imposed by Isaías on his entire
family which forbids them to admit his guilt in the
crime. Finally Luisa, his daughter-in-law, who was a
witness to the murder, breaks the silence and informs
the police. The family struggle which she and others

36

endure is one which is opposed to the responsibility
which they owe to society. The major part of the drama concerns the way in which the family reacts to the
commands of Isaías and the fear with which they are
forced to live. As one critic so aptly affirms, "el
terror que emplea el viejo campesino es de índole tota-
litaria, y la más grave de sus consecuencias es la
infidelidad en que vive esta comunidad amordazada de la
familia, la ruptura de toda convivencia civil, la impo-
sibilidad de todo proyecto y toda elección humana."[46]
Once the rule of terror has been removed, a sense of
relief and an air of melancholy, prevail. Isaías tries
to escape from the police knowing full well that he
will be killed. This he calculates will inspire guilt
in the family and they will never be able to live free
from remorse. At least this is the family's deduction
after being informed that Isaías is killed. They are
made to shoulder this responsibility as symbols of the
society. As previously mentioned, the heat is blamed
for Isaías' conduct. It is his wife Antonia who expresses this fact. One critic has indicated that Isaías'
characteristic of cold heartlessness is one which appears as a trait of revolutionary leaders in later
plays.[47]

The social implications of this play are distinct
if the entire family unit is taken as a symbol of the
larger society. Farris Anderson declares that in an
interview with José María de Quinto the latter saw this
play as a reflection of Franco's Spain "and the 'gag'
as the limitations on free expression that prevail in
Spain."[48] In fact, when Luisa speaks about the effect
that the "gag" has on all of them her words reflect the
state that an oppressed society is in, "esta mordaza
nos ahoga y algún día va a ser preciso hablar, gritar...,
si es que ese día nos quedan fuerzas... Y ese día va a
ser un día de ira y sangre..." (326). It is only when
the family or society rebels and makes itself heard
that it can enjoy freedom and self-respect.

Although La cornada does not fall into the categories of social revolution or personal rebellion, it is
a play in which Sastre voices his criticism of certain
aspects of society. Specifically in this play, he criticizes managers who hold the lives of artists in their
hands and so manipulate them that they become mere puppets, unable to function in society of their own accord.
La cornada deals specifically with the manager of a
bullfighter and Sastre reveals his disapproval of that

social system which causes the artist to yield to economic pressures and so lower his self esteem that finally he is stripped of all personal dignity. Apparently, the Spanish bourgeoisie rejected this play because
their national pastime was presented in a critical fashion.[49]

La cornada was inspired by the myth in which Saturn devours his son. Marcos, the impresario, is the
symbol of Saturn and José Alba the bullfighter is symbolic of the son. Sastre levels criticism at the society which forces José Alba to give up his medical studies for pure economic gain in the bullring; he decries
the exploitation of the bullfighter by the manager and
the manner in which the latter succeeds in destroying
the marriage of José and Gabriela, his wife. Even the
customary tardiness of the Spanish, and the importance
with which the bullfight is viewed, comes under attack
when Sastre indicates that the bullfight is the only
performance which begins on time. The play follows the
Sastrian line of investigation into the responsibility
for the tragedy which occurs. Marcos' interests are
in direct conflict with those of José's wife. Apparently
they are in conflict with the matador's as well; but he
is too weak a creature to express his true desires.
The play has a prologue in which José's death is established. The remainder of the play presents in retro-
spect the details which preceeded the death of José.
There is an epilogue over whose validity and necessity
several critics have quibbled. In the body of the play
Sastre presents the mortal fear which grips José before
the fight commences. Gabriela attempts to convince
José to renounce this profession which carries glory
and power with it and to return to her and to a life
in which he could be happy; one in which all glory and
power would be lacking. José is almost persuaded when
Marcos enters and with the unscrupulous power which he
yields over José convinces the latter to dismiss Gabriela. When José's fear overwhelms him and Marcos refuses to inspire José to do his bidding in his customary
fashion, José stabs himself, so that he will not have
to fight. At this point, Marcos induces José to seek
medical attention for his wound and then prevails upon
him to fight in spite of the wound. José is gored and
dies, not from this, but because of the self inflicted
wound. The epilogue presents Marcos as he attempts to
encourage a young café owner, Rafael Pastor (who had
suffered illusions of being a matador), to renounce his
business enterprise and to become his protégé. The

latter proves to be the mouthpiece of the dramatist as
he rejects Marcos' plea..."Pero sí sé, por lo que he
visto ya, que hay unos en esta vida que viven de la
desgracia de los otros; que se aprovechan, para vivir,
de todo lo que está en peligro, de lo que se muere...,
de todas las cosas pobres que se consumen poco a poco
... Eso también es una historia española..., ¿ verdad?
Echar a pelearse a la gente y ver los toros desde la
barrera y guardarse el dinero de los muertos..." (939-
940). Pastor is also criticizing the custom of Marcos
to substitute propaganda for truth--this is "una historia española"--wherein Marcos will fabricate a rags-to-
riches story in order to make Pastor more acceptable to
the Spanish public. Pastor utters this rejection while
he can see outside of his tavern, a beggar, a former
reject matador and protégé of Marcos. The latter totally ignores the plight of the former matador.

The problem presented by Sastre is aptly defined
by a critic who has declared that "hay un tremendo pro-
blema humano, un radical choque de personalidades y unas
dimensiones infinitamente más amplias que el tamaño de
los cuernos de un toro...pero lo que va a desarrollarse
a partir entonces, retrospectivamente, es la historia
de la despicidada invención y destrucción de una 'gloria'
taurina por un cínico e implacable apoderado, el acerado
Marcos, el hombre forjado del acero de los que juegan
con las vidas ajenas".[50] The presence of the beggar at
the end is not a detracting element as has been suggested. He is a reminder to Pastor of what Marcos' rejects
represent and is a large contributing factor which causes Pastor to be able to refuse the offers made by Marcos. In addition, the beggar's presence serves to re-
mind the spectator of the fate of these people and gives
further impetus to the strong ideological declaration
that is explicitly expressed. It should be noted that
Adolfo Marsillach, who directed the performance of La
cornada, expressed the desire to interpret the problems
which Sastre presents in such a way that they would be
clearly seen as examples of other possible situations.[51]
Consequently, although the play ends on a note of optimism, the presence of the beggar and his plea for help
from the audience is powerful enough to produce a cathar-
tic effect on the spectator.

Oficio de tinieblas cannot be categorized as a
drama of social realism but it warrants mention here in
so far as the purpose of the dramatist was to present a
socially moral problem. However, the intent of the play-

wright did not materialize into the idea that he was
attempting to project. The play begins as a drama of
social situation but develops into one of the individual characters whose personal morals are to be questioned. Sastre presents a group of characters which
includes fascists of various origins, two prostitutes
and an innocent victim who is the protégé of one of the
men. The political implications are not developed and
the social content amounts to nothing more than a series
of spoken manifestations against the war, alcoholism and
prostitution. No intricate social dialectic is presented. This play suffers from the fact that the political
characterization is not developed in such a way as to
make it meaningful to the plot. Neither are the elements of moral characterization linked sufficiently with
the political. The moral tends to obscure the political
to the point where the latter is merely incidental to
the plot. Consequently the political conception of the
play is converted into a dramatic reflexion of the moral quality of some individuals.[52] For this reason, it
is not essential to analyze further the social implications raised.

Asalto nocturno reflects more acutely than any
other play, the authentic criminal investigation which
is an essential part of Sastre's dialectics. In this
scenario a series of crimes is uncovered and the burning issue raised is where does one direct the guilt and
responsibility for each of these crimes? Although the
play is in the epic style of Brecht, the moral issue is
a social one. The succession of incidents which reflect
the eye for an eye and tooth for a tooth philosophy
causes one to stop and consider the ultimate waste of
life and suffering which these families had to endure
and the fact that at best it is the innocent who suffer
the most. From this perspective the play qualifies as
a social drama. This drama spans a period of sixty-five
years and many characters appear at different moments in
this span. The settings range from New York to a Mediterranean island where the family feud originated. The
police in New York initiate an investigation into the
murder of Professor Graffi. As it turns out, the professor is almost at the end of the line of the family
feud which began in the Mediterranean. He is the victim
of personal revenge. Carlo Graffi, the father of Professor Marcelo Graffi, had initiated the feud with the
Bosco family by his overbearing personality as the head
of the most powerful family. The specific act, which
prompted the first killing, was the rape of Marga Bosco

as a young girl by Carlo Graffi. Upon his death she
induces her brother Angelo to seek revenge by killing
Carlo's eldest son Sandro. Some years later Angelo,
finally unable to live free from the memory of his
crime, goes to Marcelo's home and discloses his identity. Marcelo is willing to let bygones be bygones but
his brother Tonio kills Angelo. Angelo's son Ugo finally hires an assassin to murder Marcelo since Tonio's
incarceration makes him unavailable. It is the police
inspector Orkin who relays the events as they occur,
tying them in with world events which occurred simultaneously. It is in this narration of world events
that the period is set.

Before Marcelo Graffi is killed he records a message on tape in which he lectures to his class about the
atomic bombings of Hiroshima and Nagasaki and the tragic
repercussions. This message reveals the relationship
between the family feud and international wars. The
message is not implicit but the suggestion is relayed.
Carlo Graffi's guilt is unquestionable but the refusal
of Marga's father through fear to confront the tyrant
at the time of his act leads to the rest of the senseless killings. The innocent victims, Sandro and Marcelo are forced to suffer for someone else's sin. Here
is a relationship to the question posed in Escuadra hacia
la muerte. Carlo Graffi "simboliza la sociedad injusta
que por no ser desarraigada a tiempo sigue viviendo y
sigue oprimiendo a los débiles".[53] Perhaps if Marga's
father had taken matters into his own hands as did
Guillermo Tell, the series of later killings might have
been averted. As it is, his refusal to act throws the
responsibility clearly on his own shoulders. The fact
that Marcelo Graffi accepts his death in order to
terminate these killings is an indication of a possible
solution and end to this family feud. Through his sacrifice the reign of hatred will possibly be concluded.
Although no specific ideology is expressed the reader
of this play still receives the socially moral message.

The plays which have been discussed here all
reveal that Sastre's theatre is one of siutations in
which the protagonist is placed in a predicament which
warrants action of some sort. Refusal to act (Marco
Bosco) results in enslavement though if action is taken
the protagonist succeeds in removing the social injustices. However, his act also results in consequences
which may involve grief and suffering. In spite of
this many of Sastre's plays end on a note of hope. It
is often the role of a specific individual which

implies this note of optimism. Specifically, Sastre has
utilized the female role in order to offset the tragic
consequences. Many an inspiration of hope has resulted
from the relationship which exists between male and female. In addition, the choice which the individual must
make before he can act, if he is going to act, relies
to a great extent on the type of individual being portrayed and the way in which the social ills have affected said individual.

FOOTNOTES TO CHAPTER II

[1]"De la 'funcionalidad social' de la tragedia", Drama y sociedad, pp. 55-56.

[2]See Sastre's reply to Eusebio García Luengo, revealed in "Sobre las formas 'sociales' del drama", Alfonso Sastre, Teatro, pp. 88-94. This first appeared in Correo Literario, (Madrid 1 de enero de 1952).

[3]Drama y sociedad, pp. 126-127.

[4]"Primer encuentro con el drama de acción social", Primer Acto, 8 (mayo-junio 1959), pp. 6-10.

[5]See Rafael Vázquez Zamora, "Autores de hoy y de mañana: Alfonso Sastre", Insula, Año 12, 130 (sept. de 1957), 10.

[6]Drama y sociedad, pp. 49-50.

[7]Ibid., pp. 47-48.

[8]See the bibliography for the list of journals in which these articles have appeared.

[9]F. García Pavón, El teatro social en España, (1895-1962) (Madrid: Ediciones Taurus, 1962), pp. 173-179.

[10]See Ricardo Doménech, "Entrevista con Alfonso Sastre", Alfonso Sastre, Teatro, p. 60.

[11]J.M. García Escudero, "Tiempo", Alfonso Sastre, Teatro, pp. 65-69.

[12]Drama y sociedad, pp. 94-97.

[13]Ibid., pp. 91-92.

[14]Farris Anderson, Alfonso Sastre, p. 33.

[15]See "Arte como construcción: manifiesto de Alfonso Sastre", _Alfonso_ _Sastre_, _Teatro_, pp. 107-114. This manifesto was reprinted in _Anatomía_ _del_ _realismo_ pp. 16-24.

[16]_Alfonso_ _Sastre_, _Teatro_, p. 111.

[17]_Alfonso_ _Sastre_, p. 84.

[18]Albert E. Bilyeu, "Alfonso Sastre...", p. 90.

[19]_Drama_ _y_ _sociedad_, pp. 113-115.

[20]_Ibid._, pp. 123-124.

[21]Leonard Pronko, "The 'Revolutionary Theatre' of Alfonso Sastre", _Tulane_ _Drama_ _Review_, 5, 2 (Dec. 1960), 111.

[22]Domingo Pérez Minik, "Se trata de Alfonso Sastre...", p. 18.

[23]_Drama_ _y_ _sociedad_, pp. 127-128.

[24]Anderson, _Alfonso_ _Sastre_, p. 36.

[25]_Ibid._, pp. 36-37.

[26]Anje Van der Naald, _Alfonso_ _Sastre_: _Dramaturgo_ _de_ _la_ _revolución_ (New York: Las Americas Publishing Co., Inc., 1973), p. 111.

[27]"Se trata de Alfonso Sastre...", p. 15.

[28]Anthony M. Pasquariello, "Alfonso Sastre: Dramatist in Search of A Stage", _The_ _Theatre_ _Annual_, No. 22 (1965-66). p. 20.

[29]Alfonso Sastre, _Obras_ _Completas_, I (Madrid: Aguilar, 1967), 216-217. All subsequent quotations from Sastre's plays will be taken from this edition.

[30]Anthony M. Pasquariello, "Censorship in the Spanish Theatre and Alfonso Sastre's The Condemned Squad", The Theatre Annual, 19 (1962), 24.

[31]Juan Villegas, "La sustancia metafísica de la tragedia y su función social: Escuadra hacia la muerte de Alfonso Sastre", Symposium, 21, 3 (Fall 1967), 258.

[32]Van der Naald, p. 54.

[33]Alfonso Sastre, pp. 107-108.

[34]Ibid., p. 109.

[35]Van der Naald, pp. 27-28. Farris Anderson also blames the weakness on the vague background which the collective movement provides for Germán's actions. Alfonso Sastre, p. 85.

[36]See D. Pérez Minik, "Se trata de Alfonso Sastre...", pp. 27-28.

[37]Ibid., pp. 25-26.

[38]Anderson, Alfonso Sastre, p. 87.

[39]J. Rodríguez Puértolas, "Tres aspectos de una misma realidad en el teatro español contemporáneo: Buero, Sastre, Olmo," Hispanófila, 2, No. 31 (1967), p. 51.

[40]Adolfo Prego, "Crítica" En la red, Teatro español 1960-1961, (Madrid: Aguilar, 1962), p. 251.

[41]Alfonso Sastre, "Autocrítica", En la red, Teatro español 1960-1961 (Madrid: Aguilar, 1962), p. 249.

[42]Anderson Alfonso Sastre, p. 86.

[43]See Eduardo Haro Tecglen, "Introducción a Alfonso Sastre", Primer Acto, 6 (enero-Feb. 1958), p. 18; García Pavón, p. 177; Giuliano, p. 180.

[44]G. Torrente Ballester, _Teatro español contemporáneo_, 2nd ed., (Madrid: Ediciones Guadarrama, 1968), p. 137.

[45]_Ibid._, p. 139.

[46]Pérez Minik, "Se trata de Alfonso Sastre...", p. 24.

[47]Pronko, "The Revolutionary Theatre of Alfonso Sastre", p. 115.

[48]_Alfonso Sastre_, p. 97.

[49]Pérez Minik, "Se trata de Alfonso Sastre...", p. 28.

[50]Rafael Vázquez Zamora, "_La cornada_ de Alfonso Sastre en El Lara," _Insula_, Año 15, 159 (feb. de 1960), p. 15.

[51]Adolfo Marsillach, "Cuaderno de dirección de _La cornada_", _Primer Acto_, 12 (enero-feb. 1960), p. 20.

[52]Angel Fernández Santos, "_Oficio de tinieblas_ de A. Sastre", _Insula_ Año 22, 244 (marzo de 1967), p. 17.

[53]Giuliano, p. 200.

CHAPTER III

THE INDIVIDUAL IN SOCIETY

In the previous chapter it has been shown that both collective rebellion and individual rebellion or self-assertion exist in Sastre's plays. Sastre's protagonists possess the freedom to act if they so desire in order to ameliorate the social or political situation. Usually this situation is determined by the way in which the society reacts to social injustice. Consequently, the individual can assert his liberty but is limited in his action by the confines of the particular society. For this reason, the protagonist has to be conscious at all times of the consequences that will be involved when he asserts himself and also has to be prepared to accept the responsibility and admit his guilt when the situation so demands. In addition to the man of action or the individual who is prepared to take action, Sastre also presents the theorist--one who spends all his time theorizing and being subjected to anger and frustration when confronted with the situation, but who nevertheless, is incapable of taking matters into his own hands in order to affect some social change. The theorist will be discussed first in the light of the various situations in which he is placed in the different dramas.

The relevant play which immediately comes to mind is Escuadra hacia la muerte. In this play Javier is presented as the philosopher who finds himself in the condemned squad for being a coward who would not obey military commands which involved violence and killings. This former professor of metaphysics is very active mentally and, because he is a pacifist, cannot accept the realities of war. In fact, he blames wars on those who are consistently prepared to become heroes. As he says, "Eso debíamos hacer, quitar a los héroes y no habría guerras." (180). Indeed, Javier had been so immersed in his professorial activities that he had not been aware that the war was so imminent. In a letter which Javier writes to his mother in his diary, he declares how unbearable life is for him with the strict maintenance of military discipline and the unnerving wait for the enemy offensive. In this same notation in his diary, he confesses to being a coward and a deserter. He philosophizes about the present predicament of the condemned squad and the possible purification which

may result from their suffering: "En realidad, todos
estamos aquí con una culpa en el corazón y un remor-
dimiento en la conciencia. Puede que éste sea el cas-
tigo que nos merezcamos y que, en el momento de morir,
seamos una escuadra de hombres purificados y dignos."
(184). He attempts to rationalize his behavior by suggesting that his guilt lies in the fact that he tried
too desperately to hold on to life rather than being
willing to give it up in battle. It is for this reason
more than any other that he is being punished. Here
Javier is not speaking of a punishment inflicted by
society but rather by God. Later on while Javier is
alone on guard duty the fear of solitude overwhelms
him and he voices the thought that this squad was condemned even before the war broke out. They consitute
"una generación estúpidamente condenada al matadero"
(190). This aspect of the original sin is echoed repeatedly by Javier. As a professor of philosophy he is
tortured by the metaphysical question of man's guilt.
He declares his preference for death rather than capti-
vity--an anticipation of his eventual suicide.

When Goban orders Javier to relieve Luis, who is on
guard duty, Javier refuses to obey. The fact that
Javier is present when Goban is killed is a direct result of his refusal to act. It is only after Adolfo
has wounded the corporal that Javier acts violently.
He does not however participate actively in the plans
that follow Goban's death. His only concern is whether
the enemy is advancing. He lives in mortal fear of
this. He advises the others not to count on him for
anything. When Adolfo questions Javier as to his plans
the latter answers that he will remain there although
Adolfo warns him that he may be shot. Javier brushes
aside this warning suggesting that this may not occur.
He declines however, to give any explanation for this
judgment. He merely reiterates his sentiment about
the role that destiny has played in their lives: "Es
inútil luchar. Está pronunciada la última palabra y
todo es inútil. En realidad, todo era inútil...desde
un principio. Y desde un principio estaba pronunciada
la última palabra. Todavía queréis luchar contra el
destino de esta escuadra...que no es solo la muerte,
como creíamos al principio..., sino una muerte infame
... ¿Tan torpes sois...que no os habéis dado cuenta
aún?" (215).

The destiny of the condemned squad is inescapable.
Javier informs Pedro that he is scientifically probing

the events which have occurred and he has reached the
conclusion that Goban's death was no fortuitous act.
Again, he repeats his conviction that it was all part
of a master plan of punishment. Goban's death was
inevitable for as long as he lived their existence was
almost happy--one of merely obeying and suffering.
They at least suffered the illusion that they were
purifying themselves and would thus ultimately be saved
in an existential manner. Goban however, allowed himself to be killed in order that they would be tortured
forever. "Estaba aquí para que lo matáramos. Y caímos
en la trampa. Por si eso fuera poco, la última opor-
tunidad, la ofensiva, nos ha sido negada. Para nosotros estaba decretada, desde no sé dónde, una muerte
sucia" (216-217). When Pedro affirms that their only
recourse is prayer, Javier counters by stating the futi-
lity of such an exercise since they are being punished
by some unknown being for an equally unknown and mysterious sin. As far as Javier is concerned, there is no
way out of this but the one which he elects, namely
suicide. Luis, the youngest of the squad feels that
Javier's action is one of self-condemnation which is
even worse. It is significant that for this man of
inaction, the one decisive act that he does commit is
one of self-annihilation. Javier's belief that Goban
deliberately allowed himself to be killed in order to
punish the others is echoed in La mordaza. (When
Isaías is killed trying to escape, the family is convinced that he deliberately had himself killed in order
to torture their consciences.)

Javier's refusal to act is coupled with his desire
to seek refuge in theorizing. This is typical of
Sastre's characters who are theorists. Javier explains
that from early childhood he seemed to be different to
the other children because he always indulged in abstract thought. This bears a strong resemblance to the
childhood of David Harko, protagonist of El pan de todos who spent much of his time reading books. "For
Javier as for David, suffering becomes an absolute
state of consciousness. Javier's companions also suffer, but each looks to his own brand of hope."[1] Here
is a character who lives tormented perpetually by the
insoluble questions which forever plague him. This
torment is an essential part of the Sastrian character
regardless of the role which he is to play. It is
noteworthy that unlike the existentialist characters
of Jean-Paul Sartre, Sastre's characters do not agonize
about which course of action they should pursue. They

49

agonize over what they have done. The typical Sastrian
character is faced with only one course of action.
Javier never considers any other path but suicide. One
can look to other plays and see that suicide is the
only path that is left open to the theorist.

Walter Fürst, Tell's father-in-law, is another such
character. In Guillermo Tell tiene los ojos tristes,
Fürst is a pure theorist. He is the caricature of the
revolutionary man.[2] Fürst is replete with revolutionary
rhetoric. He sees his role quite clearly as that of the
man who plans the strategy. The revolutionary act will
have to be undertaken by someone else. Fürst states
this implicity while speaking to one of the beggars
"Lo mío...es pensar por vosotros, compañero. Lo vuestro
..., actuar por mí. Yo pienso para que lo que vosotros
hagáis no sea un crimen. Vosotros actuaréis para que
lo que yo pienso no sea una pura filosofía, ¿entien-
des?" (613). The beggar reflects his astuteness when
he calmly retorts "Entiendo que a nosotros nos corres-
ponderá mancharnos las manos con la sangre, señor Fürst"
(613). He accedes without conviction when Fürst urges
him to call him "compañero" rather than "señor"..
Fürst responds to Tell's account of the beatings which
he suffered during incarceration, by declaring that
often one's fury is greater and one's pain is worse when
it is someone else who has physically suffered. Sastre
presents Fürst as one who takes his theorizing very
seriously. He is convinced that he is making revolution in his own way but it is obvious by Sastre's presentation of Fürst as one who considers himself a failure, that Sastre sees the revolutionary act as the only
effective way of changing the status quo. This is
clearly evident in the following dialogue:

FÜRST.＿ Haré un artículo para la hoja. Convocaré
todos los jefes de la resistencia en los cantones. Hay
que hacer una compaña de propaganda y agitación.

TELL.＿ Usted es como un profesor, señor Fürst.
Usted escribe muy bien. Los demás jefes son también
unos hombres inteligentes, ¿cómo se dice?, "intelectua-
les" o algo así. Si se reúnen harán una tertulia literaria, no una revolución (616).

Fürst continues with his theoretical tactics by holding
a meeting to plan for the revolution. When he becomes
entangled in the parliamentary processes of electing
officers for the committee Tell voices his impatience

with their idea of "action". Fürst labels him an anarchist. Sastre's revelation of irony is not lost here. Here are so called revolutionaries, supposedly wasting time with matters of procedure and daring to call someone who calls for action an anarchist. Fürst attempts to explain Tell to his comrades by stating that "no puede soportar la disciplina, el método, la burocracia." (626). However, when they need Tell, Fürst knows that they will be able to count on him to take action; for the present at any rate it is up to them to do the thinking for Tell.

When Fürst is forced by the guards to bow to the governor's hat and acclaim a long life for him his humiliation knows no bounds. He is so ashamed that he goes off to hide and finally commits suicide. However, Fürst's action does not surprise Tell who considers that like a professor, Fürst would be unable to withstand such a test. "Ellos solo saben hablar. Hablan muy bien. Se dan cuenta de los problemas. Pero nada más" (638). Tell knows Fürst will never forgive himself and his suicide only serves as an incentive for Tell's later action. Unlike Javier, Fürst does not contemplate his suicide beforehand. The fact that he sees himself as a revolutionary who has failed is what instigates his self-pity. He cannot live with this. For Fürst there is no other alternative but to take his own life. Ironically, it is at this moment that he chooses to act.

A third prime example of the theorist who is unable to live with himself after not being able to withstand police torture is Leo of En la red. Leo, Celia's husband, is caught in a police dragnet and is incarcerated and tortured. However, he is released and without thinking that he might be followed, goes directly to the appointed hiding place where Celia and other political activists are entrenched. It is obvious to Pablo that Leo was freed because he had revealed what the police wished to hear. Leo was unable to withstand the torture and tells Celia that he cannot forgive her and the others for not warning him; thus, causing him to fall into the police trap. He is so ashamed at having broken under torture that he is quite prepared to die. In fact for him death is preferable to torture. He blames himself for not having resisted the torture but Celia understands what he is. She attempts to explain to Pablo exactly what type of person Leo is. "No estaba preparado para eso. El es un escritor. Lo

51

ha dado todo por esta causa. Se puso de este lado, enfrentándose con todo..." (846). Leo is fully aware that he is not truly an activist--he is merely a writer but the cause is one for which everyone should work. He tries to explain this to Pablo.

LEO.___ Yo...no soy un hombre de acción. Trate de entenderlo de una vez.

PABLO.___ ¿Por qué se metió en esto?

LEO.___ Porque "esto" es una cosa de todos. No solo de los hombres de acción. (849)

When Pablo hands Leo his safe conduct papers with which he can leave the country, Leo shows his hurt. He feels that he is scorned and considered utterly useless by the organization. He refuses to go away, maintaining his preference for death over flight or captivity. Consequently, he destroys the documents. It is no surprise therefore that when the police arrive Leo deliberately rushes out to the terrace, where he is machinegunned by the police. He does this because he is well aware of his own weakness and is afraid that under further torture he will divulge privileged information. His only recourse is the one that he takes. For Leo there is no other alternative. He is totally committed to the cause but physically he cannot resist the torture like the true political activists. Leo is guided by his intellect which tells him that he should join the revolutionary cause but his intellect is no match for his physical weakness. Like Fürst and Javier, his "action" results in self-destruction.

Prólogo patético is yet another play in which reference is made to the theorist as opposed to the man of action. When Oscar is caught by the police, Beltrán and Pablo discuss Oscar's position in the movement. Oscar's refusal to divulge any information to the police is seen in the light that he is not "un teórico". "Un teórico es un hombre que, a cada momento, puede cambiar, sin morir, de teoría. Oscar ha puesto en el juego de su existencia, no simplemente sus palabras... un teórico hubiera contado todo lo que supiera y más" (90). These two revolutionaries reflect the low esteem in which the theorist is held by political activists. When Oscar returns to the group's hideout after he is set free by the police, Pablo is prepared to have him disassociate himself from the group: "Oscar, te pido

que no continúes. Si lo prefieres, te lo ordeno. Veo
que te has dedicado a pensar. Todo eso es malsano. El
partido necesita, ahora más que nunca, hombres de acción.
El pensamiento es un lastre..., por ahora. Luego, ya
veremos a la hora de justificar lo que hagamos. Siempre
habrá un filósofo o un imbécil que nos justifique..."
(93). Oscar, however, has already decided on his course
of action. He is no longer concerned with the party because of its violent tactics. The supposed death of his
brother has been responsible for his change in attitude.
It is for this reason that he kills Pablo since he blames
him for the supposed death of Julio. Oscar differs
somewhat from Javier and Fürst in that he is prepared
to act. Although he is a "thinker" he is not strictly
speaking a theorist. His role lies somewhere between
the activist and the theorizer. He is committed to act
but cannot accept the shedding of innocent blood. For
this reason, he kills Pablo, whom he considers responsible for the bloodshed. However, once he realizes
that Julio is alive and that Pablo's death is meaning-
less he accepts his responsibility and guilt. Oscar's
misery now is that he deems himself useless to the
cause declaring that men like Pablo are what the revolution needs. He decides to suffer for the cause and
calmly awaits the arrival of the police. Oscar has
found his peace. He can now serve the revolution by
suffering for it. Oscar is typical of the Sastrian
character who agonizes over what he has done. He grie-
ves for those who have suffered but does what he considers to be absolutely essential to the cause.

Guillermo Tell is the most striking example of the
Sastrian character who becomes a reluctant anarchist.
Unlike his father-in-law Fürst, he is primarily a man
of action; yet he is not a political activist in any
form. From Sastre's presentation of Tell it is evident
that an emerging theme concerns the aloof individual
and the lack of communication between him and his society. Pérez Minik states that "Alfonso Sastre nos está
afirmando siempre que necesitamos establecer un equilibrio, una solidaridad, una comunión en el seno de la
existencia humana, entre la vida social y la privada.
Tenemos que evitar esta alienación a que está sometido
el hombre, que no la resuelven las revoluciones políticas o sociales, aunque la revolución sea su primer paso."[3] As demonstrated, Tell refutes the role of the
theorist in the revolution. This does not make him an
advocate of violent rebellion. On the contrary, he is
essentially a man of peace. After his arrest and torture

Tell displays total lack of interest in any exercise of
rebellion. He is a family man and this is what is of
utmost importance to him. "Yo no me meteré en nada,
señor Fürst. Estoy harto. Quiero volver a casa, a mi
trabajo. Quiero estar en paz" (616). Consequently, he
refuses Fürst's invitation to attend the political meeting. If Tell displays any ideological attitude, it is
towards pacifism. This is the man, however, who finds
himself as the reluctant liberator of his country. He
is not happy with his social environment but it is finally Fürst's distress and humiliation which propel Tell
towards the act of shooting the arrow through the governor's hat. Fürst understands Tell's disposition, because he tells his political comrades that when the time
comes for action Tell "saltará, aparecerá entre nosotros.
Y matará si es preciso. Incendiará casas. Hará todo
lo que haya que hacer. Parecerá un suicida. Estará en
la vanguardia, en la primera línea, en la fuerza de choque. Le tocará lo más peligroso y lo hará con alegría.
Y si es preciso, hará algo grande. A nosotros, ahora,
nos toca pensar por él" (626-627). Here is a classic
example of dramatic irony. Not only does Tell kill
because he has to, but he is all alone when the moment
arrives, and does not do it with joy but with great
sadness and cold fury since he loses his beloved son.

Tell's sadness sets him apart form the rest of
society. According to one commentary, he "is a lonely
hero who stands aloof from both a tyrannized society
and an ineffective revolutionary movement."[4] The only
people to whom Tell truly relates are his wife and son.
After the loss of his son and the death of the governor
his aloofness from the rest of the society becomes more
profound. When he needed the people's support, no one
came to aid him. He laments his solitary position in
the society:

TELL.__ ¡No era preciso que mi hijo muriera! (Los
otros bajan la cabeza. No se atreven a decir nada.)
Walty y yo nos encontramos solos. ¿Dónde estaban esos
que ahora quieren verme? ¿Qué hacían? ¿Dormían en sus
habitaciones? ¿O fumaban un cigarrillo tranquilamente?
Unos habían dado un beso a sus hijos y se habían echado
a dormir. Otros..., qué me importa... Al despertarse
se encontraron viviendo en un país libre. A mí me parece muy bien. Me alegro por ellos, que han conseguido
la libertad a tan poca costa.... Pero a mí que me dejen
en paz. Es lo único que pido. Que me perdonen si no
estoy con ellos. ¿Qué más puedo decir? (653).

Tell informs them that he does not consider himself to be the liberator of the country. He was forced to act in a certain way and if by chance the country was liberated at the same time, that has nothing to do with him. Tell's son becomes the sacrificial lamb of the revolution. Tell acts in a critical moment and like all of Sastre's protagonists he suffers deep personal grief. Before he acted he knew of the chance that his son would be killed, but he took the only course that was open to him. Now his isolation is more profound because he was prepared to die--not kill his son. The governor seemed to know that Tell's weakness was the deep familial bond that united him to Walty, his son, and Hedwig his wife. Apparent here is the fact that society can cause grief and suffering because of deep familial bonds. (This is echoed in El pan de todos when David Harko is forced to choose between the revolution and his mother.) Walty shows typical youthful hope in his fellow man. He believes that the spectators are suffering with Tell and himself. Tell with his greater knowledge of man is not so sure. Walty accuses his father of not having faith in anyone. Walty is too young to know what one can and cannot expect of one's fellow man.

The only moment in which Tell displays any violence is after accidentally killing Walty. He kills the governor and exhorts the people to tear the governor's body into pieces. He explodes for the first and last time. "¡Despedazad ese cuerpo! ¡Rompedlo en mil pedazos! ¡Que yo pueda coger su cabeza de los pelos y estrellarla contra la pared! ..."(651). Tell's feeling of isolation from the onlookers is a reflection of the fact that usually one stands alone when in trouble. When the people offer to erect a sanctuary in his memory after his death, Tell responds with the statement that nothing will be important then. This existence is what matters and he has killed his own son. Sastre, through the character Melchtal, declares that it is this fact that makes Tell's tragedy a noble one. Sastre here is defending his denouement. As the play ends Hedwig has to lull Tell to sleep with a fairy tale. It is only with the removal of reality that Tell will be able to continue living. Tell's faith in his society seems to have been shattered. He is Sastre's loneliest creature and most sympathetic. Farris Anderson declares that in this play it is "the individual character rather than the social context, that is insufficiently developed."[5] This must be refuted since it is Tell the individual who becomes the tragic figure. His tragedy is plausible; for even

though Tell has not appeared a great deal, quantitative-
ly speaking, his presentation is remarkably well delineated. His suffering is acute, his loneliness is
moving and Tell the individual provokes great sympathy.
He is presented with great sensitivity. Tell acts because of what he feels, not for what he thinks. This
perhaps is why it is so easy to empathize with him
rather than with Fürst and his colleagues. According
to one critic, Tell "es la creación más conmovedora
y más bella de todos los personajes que hacen papel en
el teatro revolucionario del autor."[6]

In _En la red_, both Celia and Pablo are the activists as opposed to Leo the thinker. They both work
actively for the cause and both seem to have important
roles among the clandestine group. Their strength of
purpose and tenacity contrast greatly with Leo's lack
of courage. The clandestine individual is completely
cut off from the rest of society. His existence is
therefore abnormal. "El hombre clandestino se encuen-
tra en una situación anormal, antisocial."[7] This type
of existence is the antithesis to what anyone should
be leading. The necessity for distrust is such that
both Celia and Leo suspect Pablo of being a police
informer. The conditions under which these clandestine
individuals must live almost deprive them of any humanity. The irony is that among other things they are
supposedly fighting for more humane conditions. The
loyalty to the cause demands such secrecy that Celia
fails to warn her husband Leo of the police dragnet and
consequently he is arrested and tortured. Celia wil-
lingly allows her husband to endure such suffering and
humiliation whilst she maintains her fidelity to the
social cause. Anderson indicates the paradox of the
clandestine situation when he maintains that "the characters act in a fraternity but are forced to live in
isolation--from the world and from each other. Tenderness and trust are luxuries which these revolutionaries
cannot afford."[8] Celia tells Pablo rather abruptly that
according to the dictates of the organization "cuanto
menos sepamos los unos de los otros, mejor"(803).After Leo
arrives at the hideout, sick with shame and pain, Celia
upbraids him for having risked their security by coming
there. The social cause is her most important consideration. She tells him he could have gone to a hotel
for the night rather than risk coming there. Celia
attempts to explain to Pablo at the beginning of the
play how they must function within the organization.
They must subject their personalities and emotions to

the cause. She warns him "no puede soportar esta inmovilidad. Ya ve, este es nuestro pobre heroísmo. Hacer
como si no existiéramos" (808). What is admirable is
that both Celia and Pablo possess the necessary fortitude with which to endure this existence. Leo, unfortunately, does not. The social issue here completely
transcends the personal. This is evident once more
when Celia tells Pablo she wants to believe in him but
they have been taught so well to be careful of where
they place their trust that she confesses "...pero ya
no puedo creer en nadie" (812).

The other couple who are in hiding are Tayeb and
his wife Aíescha. Tayeb has been pursued to such an
extent that he only feels safe when his back is in a
corner. Tayeb also reveals to Pablo his mistrust of
everyone.

> Todo el mundo puede ser policía. Casi todo el
> mundo lo es. ¡Perseguidores! Los perseguidos
> somos muy pocos. Así que...llegan a cazarnos
> siempre. ¡Antes o después! Hay que tener mucho
> cuidado. Un cuidado exquisito. Yo lo tengo. Por
> la calle me gusta ir de prisa, moverme mucho.
> Claro, es cosa de experiencia. Así no se pueden
> fijar. Pero además si disparan, puede que no
> acierten. También yendo de prisa...es posible que
> el que venga detrás no lo alcance a uno. A veces
> hasta hay que correr, y se consigue que nos pierdan
> de vista. Como ve, es completamente distinto estar
> en unahabitación que ir por la calle. No tiene
> nada que ver lo uno con lo otro. (819).

Even though his wife Aíescha has been brutally treated
by the police she still hopes that she will not die
before her people are liberated. When Celia will not
permit Tayeb to read the newspapers he agitatedly suspects that there is bad news which Celia wishes to keep
from him. He in fact becomes hysterical and Pablo has
to use force in order to tranquilize him. The pressure
of living this clandestine existence has rendered Tayeb
a nervous wreck while his wife is a physical wreck. The
question that arises here is whether the pursuit of the
liberation is worth all this suffering. Through the
positive demeanor of Pablo and Celia at the end, it is
apparent that Sastre's answer to this is in the affirma-
tive. The total effect of the clandestine existence is
one which breeds mistrust between partisans and family
alike. This is not the type of life which society

intended for one. However, the social situation in
this case is one which breeds exactly this type of
mistrust and suspicion and forces the individual into
a furtive way of life. It is clear that in this play
the social cause eclipses the personal relationships.
The individual here is pitted against a political status
quo which is deemed unjust and his existence amounts
to a persistent struggle against oppression.

In Tierra roja, Sastre is concerned with the com-
radeship evidenced in a mass effort. This contrasts
sharply with the tragic isolation witnessed in Tell and
characters in some of the other plays. When Pedro is
about to be evicted his cause is taken up first by Pablo
who in turn wins the participation of practically all
the miners. Before Pablo's effort to win the miner's
assistance, Pedro does experience loneliness. Pablo
cannot accept the resignation of Pedro and Inés. He
believes that some action on the part of the miners
could lead to a more positive attitude. He loses some
of his inhibitions, after imbibing somewhat, and attempts
to prick the consciences of fellow miners. Pablo declares his outrage and disbelief in the calm acceptance
of the miners. It is at this point that an old miner
relates the tragic consequences which they suffered
when they attempted to strike once before "...nuestras
mujeres y nuestros hijos fueron recogidos por familias
solidarias de nuestra lucha, fuera de la comarca...Nos
quedamos los hombres solos. Estuvimos dos meses de
invierno en huelga. Tuvimos muertos de hambre y de
frío. También tuvimos muertos en las refriegas" (366).
It is no wonder that these men are not willing to stage
another protest. The poor man is no match for the
capitalist company. Nevertheless, Pablo succeeds in
mustering their support. Hopeless as their situation
may seem, they still have the fortitude to try to ameliorate their unjust social conditions. It is obvious
that if they themselves do not attempt to change their
social status that society--in this case the mining
company--is not going to do it for them. Consequently,
one can interpret the mining company as symbolic of the
larger society against whom the poor individual is pitted.
A collective effort may succeed in affecting some change
but an individual effort will be totally wasted. Sastre
points out, however, that be the effort individual (as
in the case of Tell), or collective (as it is here),
sacrifice is inevitable. One must be prepared to suffer in order for conditions to be improved.

It is perhaps significant that in each case, the

individual who undertakes the task of coercing the
miners into taking action, is always youthful. It is
youth coupled with an ignorance of the existing system
which permits the individual to question the inevitabi-
lity of the injustice. Once the individual is familia-
rized with the system and is no longer youthful, his
resignation and easy acceptance are almost predestined.
It is clearly indicated that once one has experienced
and submitted to this kind of life, one's ability to
question and resist becomes inert. It is only through
coercion that the apathy can be counteracted and the
individual activated. The youthful Pedro, the young
Pablo and Joven all reflect the above mentioned characteristics of the young individuals. The older Pedro
and Pablo as well as the "viejos" in the tavern all
reflect the traits of the experienced and acquiescent
individual. The individual in Tierra roja is struggling
against "an oppressive economic system which prevents
man's self-realization as a human being; it reduces him
to insignificance among the creatures and things of the
world. The existential and social evils of such a system are inseparable. Humanity's task must be the esta-
blishment of a society which will allow every man to
leave 'a mark in the earth'."9 In spite of the apparent
hopelessness of this circle of events Joven succeeds in
instilling some hope into the mature Pablo:

JOVEN.__ Pero ahora es distinto. Ahora tenemos
compañeros. Usted no se irá de aquí.

PABLO.__ (Dice gravemente.) Escucha, muchacho...
Esa historia ya ha ocurrido...No va a empezar otra vez...
Fue sangrienta..., inútil... y tan sombría que... todavía hay noches en que no puedo dormir...(Se tapa los
ojos con las manos. Murmura con angustia.) ¡Para nada!

JOVEN.__ (Con entusiasmo.) Para nada no, señor
Pablo... Para que esta noche haya podido llegar yo aquí
y decirle... que ahora todo es distinto y que... si
corriera otra vez la sangre de los mineros, se notaría
esa sangre en todo el país..., y que si eso ocurre...
miles de obreros que usted no conoce abandonarían las
fábricas..., y llegaría la noticia a los campos y los
campesinos mirarían hacia aquí, y los estudiantes sal-
drían a las calles, a pedir justicia, frente a la
Policía..., y mucha gente que hoy está tranquila y
satisfecha se pondría pálida de miedo... (Un silencio.
PABLO parece meditar.)

PABLO.__ (Con un extraño gesto.) Es posible (408).

Pablo decides at this moment that he will not be turned
out of his home without a struggle. He is fully aware
of the possible consequences of suffering and death
but the important element here is that his air of hopeless resignation has been lifted. Apathy breeds hopelessness but the will to assert oneself implies some
change. The message clearly is that this latter aspect
is what matters, for it is only by the individual's
self-assertion that the injustices of society will be
effectually removed.

The other example of collective effort is presented
in Muerte en el barrio. Here one of the isolated figures is seen in the person of Luis, a minor character.
Yet Luis' ostracism, because of tuberculosis from which
he suffers, points to a criticism of that society which
seeks to avoid this individual rather than attempting
to improve his social as well as physical condition.
In this system the individual becomes isolated because
of neglect or indifference. The other solitary individual is Dr. Sanjo. The medical students utter expressions of disgust with Sanjo's behaviour and are determined that when their time comes, they will not act
like him. They think that Sanjo should be taught a
lesson concerning his negligent attitude. Dr. Sanjo,
however, has his own criticisms of the social medical
system. His problem is that no one else seems to care
about the unfortunate position in which he finds himself. His ostracism is evident in his pathetic appeal
for assistance.

SANJO.__ (Se vuelve a todos.) ¡Déjenme! ¡Déjenme.
irme de aquí! (El cerco se estrecha. SANJO mira
aterrado a su alrededor.) Dejen que me vaya... Es
posible que yo haya cometido algún error. ¡No se!
Denúncienme... Yo daré mis razones, mis..., mis excusas.
A veces me pongo enfermo... Y necesito... salir de la
clínica... Los pasillos me ahogan..., estoy mal... Soy
..., me siento desgraciado... ¡Tengo miedo! ¡Una guar-
dia... me da horror! ¡Me angustia esperar allí   cer-
rado! Esperar, ¿qué? ¡Puede llegar todo! ¡Un hombre
con el cráneo abierto..., sangre...!   Yo no quería de-
dicarme a la clínica... Quería investigar..., pero
necesitaba dinero..., vivir... Me vi metido en el hospital... Empecé a beber... (Grita.) ¡Les ruego que me
dejen! ¡Déjenme salir! ¡Se lo ruego a todos! ¡Déjenme! (Va hacia la puerta. En ella están vestidas de
negro, inmóviles, casi rígidas, JUANA, MARIA, y SOFIA.

60

<u>No dicen nada</u>. <u>Como sin querer le cierran el paso</u>.
<u>Se vuelve</u>.) ¡Alguien tiene que ayudarme! (<u>Ve a</u>
<u>GENOVEVA</u>.) ¡Usted!   ¡Usted me conoce, hemos traba-
jado juntos! ¡Dígales que me dejen salir de aquí!
(580-581).

Despite this desperate call for help, Sanjo remains un-
aided, and completely ostracized, until he is killed
by Arturo. Sastre attempts to mitigate Sanjo's lack of
responsibility by injecting the socially unjust reasons
which have caused Sanjo's irresponsible attitude. "Dr.
Sanjo's irresponsibility emerges as an aspect of a
larger social injustice to which the working people are
subject. For those people the doctor's behaviour becomes symbolic of a social and legal system which, from
the view point of the poor, is criminally inadequate."[10]

This leads one to consideration of the individuals
who have reached the limit of their social sufferings
and are prepared to attack the doctor for his crime.
They too commit a crime; but Sastre's implication is
that they are justified in committing this crime because
the conditions demand some sort of violent action. The
injustices which these characters suffer are treated
collectively with the exception of Luis, Sanjo and
Juana. Juana's problem will be discussed later.

Luisa of <u>La mordaza</u> is one female character who
does not become the victim of an oppressor. Luisa's
character is more strongly delineated than those of
her husband Juan and his brothers. From the first Act
of the play, Luisa stands up to her tyrannical father-
in-law Isaías. This in turn makes Juan nervous. He is
terrified of his father and is afraid of the repercussions which Luisa's frankness may cause. When Isaías
insults Luisa, Juan is too weak to rise to her defense.
Isaías cannot understand why Juan is incapable of sub-
jecting his wife to his authority. Juan, however, has
been a weak character, obviously subjected for years
by his father; so it is not strange that he should
marry a woman of stronger character. Luisa risks being
ostracized by the rest of the family when she resolves
to expose Isaías. However, she has sufficient strength
of character to be able to overcome this situation. She
is like the lone individual Tell who confronts the governor. She is aware of the possible consequences but
once she has resolved to act, she never waivers. Luisa
is the only one of Sastre's female characters who has
this role. She is the only one besides Isaías who displays any <u>voluntad</u> or <u>ánimo</u>. As far as Luisa is con-

61

cerned, Isaías does not warrant the respect which he demands. The fact that he has made advances even to her ·is another factor which causes her to stand up to him. Although Isaías threatens to kill her if she should expose his crime, she is prepared to take her chances and defy him. Her defiance pays off for the family is finally freed of Isaías' autocratic rule. She is the only female liberator apart from Celia of En la red in all of Sastre's work.

Isaías the oppressor is reminiscent of Governor Gessler in Guillermo Tell tiene los ojos tristes, of the corporal in Escuadra hacia la muerte, of the mining company in Tierra roja, of the police in En la red, Prólogo patético and of the communist party in El pan de todos. In these social dramas, Sastre presents the oppressor either as an individual or some collective force. Similarly, he presents the victim as individual members of a society or as the collectively oppressed in society. In addition, the woman is depicted either in a subservient role to her male counterpart or as the driving force behind the male. Luisa of La mordaza is an exception.

Before discussing the female role in detail let us first discuss the male individual as a victim of society. Escuadra hacia la muerte involves the victimization of the five soldiers first by some undisclosed source--a predestined force of oppression--and then by the person of Goban himself. As victims, each soldier reacts in a different manner. Javier, the philosopher, resorts to suicide. Luis would welcome death rather than live to endure society for the rest of his life. Andrés, like so many of Sastre's victims, chooses to drown his problems in alcohol. Alcohol plays a significant role in abating the miseries which many victims are forced to endure. Dr. Sanjo of Muerte en el barrio also chooses this path to oblivion. For the miners in Tierra roja, Arturo and his friends in Muerte en el barrio, and Germán and others in El cubo de la basura, the tavern becomes not only a place for social gatherings but also a source for drowning one's problems.

Even Sastre's asocial plays present individuals who are in some way victims of their society. Ana Kleiber depicts a woman Ana who succumbs to certain social evils. Oficio de tinieblas, too, deals with female characters who are victims of a group of parasitical males. These men represent the society in which they live and their social disgraces involve debauchery.

62

They victimize not only Miguel but the women with whom they associate. Asalto nocturno, which deals with the family feuds of the Graffi and Bosco families, also reflects the eldest Graffi as the initial oppressor of the other villagers, particularly the women who are victims of his cruelty and licentiousness. La cornada, portrays the oppressor Marcos and the oppressed José Alba and Gabriela. Gabriela's role as the wife is shown by Marcos to be subservient to the profession of José Alba. As far as Marcos is concerned the husband-wife relationship is of no importance. Both Gabriela and José Alba, as well as the former bullfighter Ricardo Platero, are portrayed as victims of a society in which people like Marcos control the lives of other individuals. The mutual dependency between Alba and Marcos completely outweighs the relationship between Alba and Gabriela. This becomes a question of the exploiter (Marcos) and the exploited (Alba).

El pan de todos portrays an individual in a particularly difficult position. Sastre begins this play with an exposé of David Harko's deep political conviction. He is so totally committed to the revolution that he exhorts his comrades to conduct themselves in a manner expected of revolutionaries and further declares that there is going to be a purge of the party in order to ferret out any traitors: "La situación en que hemos encontrado algunos sectores de obreros o campesinos y los informes directos que hemos recibido de viejos combatientes de la ciudad y del campo, nos hacen ver la necesidad de una investigación más a fondo y, probablemente, de una depuración de alcance nacional... No estamos dispuestos a consentir que una minoría de criminales entorpezca la marcha de la Revolución... no vamos a vacilar, digo, en hacer un escarmiento ejemplar... Yo os pido que nos transmitáis, a tráves de vuestros comités, vuestras informaciones y denuncias..." (231-232). There is no question about David's commitment. He has participated in forming this new society and at all costs he intends to see it succeed. The social issues are of utmost importance to David. He intends to see to it that everyone receives his share of bread. No one should have to suffer hunger. This was one of the resolutions of the revolutionary party.

It is not surprising that David is determined that Pedro Yudd, whom he suspects of profiteering with the people's bread, should be caught and punished. The tragedy is that David's mother Juana has accepted money illegally from Yudd and consequently is now in a compromising situation. Juana is motivated entirely by familial concerns. She has done this for David's benefit, unknown to him. Thus, we see the conflicting situation of these two individuals; the one motivated by social issues and the other by familial needs. It is clear that the emphasis which Sastre places on the social values here is relative. According to one source "he shows that the revolutionary ideal is inevitably subject to contamination by individual egos and that a political system can be established and defended only through a pragmatic distortion of truth."[11]

David's wife Marta describes her husband as a man who is consumed by the revolution. She forsees that he will never live to enjoy a ripe old age. She declares that "él tiene como un demonio dentro que no lo deja... Para él siempre habrá algo que hacer más allá, y no sé si podrá resistirlo" (235). Marta realizes that her husband's ideological commitment is too intense. It borders on the abnormal. It appears that in this play the social cause transcends the familial bonds. In spite of this fact, David cannot accept his betrayal of his mother. He has failed, for he could not even prevent his own mother from betraying the revolution. The sacrifice which he is expected to make for the party proves to be too much of a burden for him. He silently permits his mother to be executed without lifting a finger to aid her; but David is not as callous as he may at first seem to be. He is merely an unfortunate being who has been blinded by an inhumane ideology. His only solution is suicide. Typical of Sastre's characters like Fürst and Javier, David is unable to live with his conscience and sees no other means of escape--for escape he must from the unjust society which has placed him in such a position where he is forced to choose between the state and his mother. No just society would make such demands. David like Tell is a solitary figure; he too has "los ojos tristes". His sickliness as a child set him apart from the other children. His father had turned to politics in an attempt to improve the family's social position. According to Paula, David's aunt, the revolution brought nothing but fear and anguish to that home. The irony is that at this point Paula does not foresee how much more pain and anguish the revolution will cause for the family. A further ironic point is that Juana, David's mother, only takes the money from Yudd because as she perceives it, the revolution has failed. Yet her son David who also sees the "impending" failure views his mother's act as one element in that failure. Consequently, they

both see the failure of the revolution to correct the
social ills, but each of them reacts differently because
of the particular way in which each views the revolution.
The deaths of both Juana and David reflect this basic
difference in their view of society. The society is
so important to David that the guilt which he feels for
being responsible for his mother's death is too much to
bear. Juana, on the other hand, is at peace as she
faces death. She never had David's reverence for society and she is better able to cope with her situation
than is David. Consequently, David dies tormented;
Juana dies peacefully.

The position of Germán in El cubo de la basura
"reflects his commitment to people as individuals."[12]
Germán declares: "Es que yo no creo en la 'injusticia
social', señor Tomás, ya lo sabe. Yo no creo en más
injusticia que en la que cometan conmigo. Y mi caso
no puede resolverlo ni un Sindicato ni la Policía.
Cada uno tiene que hacer su justicia, me parece a mí"
(120). Germán is not being merely selfish. He cares
deeply for those who are close to him. It is significant that Luis admires Germán's attitude in this respect.
Germán stands out form the other characters only because of this attitude. It is as if Germán existed outside of any social laws or confines. The individual is
of prime concern here. Germán is nothing more than an
anarchist. The injustice which Germán sets out to era-
dicate--the seduction and abandonment of Julia--leads
to the consideration of the victimization of the female
in society.

The sexual deception suffered by women is a frequent occurrence in Sastre's plays. Although no women
are portrayed in Escuadra hacia la muerte, the violation
of Pedro's wife by enemy soldiers is forever present in
his mind. All of his action and decisions reflect his
reaction to his wife's rape. Sastre further presents
women who are forced to suffer the humiliation of being
sexually attacked or victimized. Even the early play
Cargamento de sueños presents a situation in which Frau
is killed for her infidelity to her lover. The social
restoration of the fallen woman can be achieved by
marriage. This is true of David Harko's wife in El pan
de todos; Germán attempts to restore Julia socially by
killing her seducer. The "forastero" threatened Isaías'
life because the latter had attempted to violate his
wife and had then killed her and their child. The Bosco-
Graffi feud is initiated by Carlo Graffi's violation of

Marga Bosco. Ana Kleiber epitomizes the fallen woman and the theme amounts to the attempt by Alfredo to restore her socially by his purifying love. In Oficio de tinieblas, Isméne, a prostitute, is the only one who treats Miguel with any kindness. In fact Miguel's dilemma as a murderer involves the murder of a prostitute during a night of debauchery by victimizing males. The prostitute, or the fallen woman, is a frequent female role in Sastre's theatre. Women are also portrayed as the suffering wife, the moral supporter, and as the woman whose motherhood transcends her role as wife. These relationships will be discussed fully in the following chapter.

From an examination of Sastre's portrayal of the individual in society, it becomes apparent that the role played is predetermined by whether the individual is a person of action or a theorist; an oppressor or a victim. The manner in which the individual views society is also of great importance. The individual adheres to social rules if he sees justice in society. However, he will take matters into his own hands if society prohibits any sort of justice for the poor or oppressed person. It is for this reason that at times the personal relationships transcend the social cause while in other situations the social issues dominate the personal or human relationship. In the examination of this theme one also sees the lonely or isolated individual as opposed to those who are collectively inert. Sastre presents collective action in order to combat one aspect of social injustice which is perhaps of a nature where individual effort would result in failure. For in the individual who acts there has to be a commitment to the cause and a deep feeling for one's fellow man. A lack of commitment results in a state of despair which causes the individual to live a life devoid of meaning and self-dignity. The individual who singlehandedly ameliorates his society has to be an exceptional character. Tell stands apart from all others in his society. Pablo and Celia are singular beings. Luisa makes Isaías' sons and wife look like mere puppets. When the individual does not possess the necessary requirements to be a man of action, he seeks to escape from the absence of a meaningful existence either by committing suicide or losing himself in an alcoholic stupor.

FOOTNOTES TO CHAPTER III

[1] Lynette H. Seator, "A Study of the Plays of Alfonso Sastre: Man's Struggle for Identity in a Hostile World", Diss. University of Illinois 1972, p. 44.

[2] See Van der Naald, p. 83.

[3] "Se trata de Alfonso Sastre...", p. 26.

[4] Seator, p. 199.

[5] Anderson, Alfonso Sastre, p. 87.

[6] Van der Naald, pp. 87-88.

[7] Ibid., p. 89.

[8] Anderson, Alfonso Sastre, p. 112.

[9] Ibid., p. 111.

[10] Ibid., p. 101.

[11] Anderson, Alfonso Sastre, p. 86.

[12] Seator, p. 56.

CHAPTER IV

MALE-FEMALE RELATIONSHIPS

In the preceeding chapter it was ascertained that the individual in Sastre's theatre plays a specific role. At times both male and female persons denote certain roles in society. The female role has been used sometimes to counteract a tragic situation; at other times it is supportive of the male role and yet at others it portrays a victim of the male and also of society. Generally, the male is the dominant character in the Sastrian theatre and most frequently the protagonist is male. Consequently, it would appear that the female role is always subordinate to the male. This is not necessarily so. The manner in which Sastre depicts certain female characters quite often detracts from the male character. In certain portrayals of the woman, her situation accentuates the injustices inherent in society; and it is not merely a reflection of the way Sastre views the female in society but a reflection of the true nature of society.

In three of Sastre's plays the woman is given an equally important or more important role than is the man. These plays are Ana Kleiber, En la red and La mordaza. It is of utmost importance to indicate here that in spite of the larger number of male protagonists in the other plays, the role played by the females, and the relationships which exist between man and woman, greatly influence the outcome of the situation in which the protagonist is placed. Since Ana Kleiber is the only play which portrays a love theme it will be discussed last.

The two female characters who initiate action are Celia (of En la red) and Luisa (of La mordaza.) Celia stands out both in her relationship with Leo, her husband, and with Pablo, a political activist. In spite of Pablo's strength of character and purpose Celia is an equal match for him. As the play opens, Celia warns Pablo that others who have spoken as courageously as he, succumbed in the end because they couldn't stand the torture. In the opening scene, Celia's fortitude is revealed. It will not come as a surprise that at the end she will complacently go off to face police torture. She is clearly in command and displays authority that is expected of a leader. When Pablo attempts to praise her physical attributes in order to alleviate the tension, Celia brusquely brushes aside his compliment, and in a very business-like manner attempts to turn the conversation to less personal matters. When Pablo mockingly tells Celia that he does not know whether he can tolerate her orders she calmly tells him, "Si no lo soporta, puede abrir la puerta y salir; márchese" (805). Although Celia's manner is authoritarian, Sastre nevertheless imbues her with femininity as is reflected in Pablo's remarks. She is not a cold woman by any means. She is in fact afraid to allow her feelings to overcome her intellect and purpose of mind. Indeed Pablo's admiration and respect for Celia are indubitable.

> PABLO.___ ...Me alegro de que me haya permitido, por fin, hablar. (Ella sonríe.) Estos tres días me ha mantenido usted a distancia. Estaba, lo confieso, un poco atemorizado.

> CELIA.___ ¿Ha tenido miedo de mí?

> PABLO.___ Un..., un respeto enorme. Estaba demasiado seria. Hasta el punto de que deseaba escapar lo antes posible. (808).

Pablo confessed further that when he was informed that he would have to go into hiding, and that he would have to take orders from a woman, he was prepared to object. He therefore decided to dress himself in a manner that would appeal to an attractive woman. Pablo, here, betrays the typical male reaction to a female companion. In fact Pablo even attempts to obtain from Celia, her place of domicile so that "someday" he could see her again. "Me gustaría mucho volver a verla. Le haría una visita muy cortés. Puede que incluso afectuosa. Le daría las gracias y hasta es posible que me pusiera sentimental. (Un silencio.) Así que... una cita de amor." (810). This insinuation of a possible love affair between the two is never developed.

Love in Sastre's plays is subservient to the social issues. In this play, there is no room for further development of a love affair because of Leo, Celia's husband. Even though Leo is killed at the end, there is still no further suggestion of the development of any personal sentiment. The only element that is discernible is the courage and strength of Pablo and Celia as they are taken away by the police. As she is cruelly pushed from Leo's body she seeks refuge in Pablo's arms and sobs. This is her first and only display of emotions. It is interesting to note that Pablo and Celia

are handcuffed to each other and that even though in
the beginning her strength seemed to be indomitable,
she does betray her emotions. Pablo, however, remains
resolute and Celia has to seek in Pablo a reaffirmation
of her courage. This is one example of the way in which
Sastre graces Celia with a feminine quality which otherwise would be undermined had her spirit not been broken
momentarily at Leo's death. This is also one way in
which Sastre maintains her credibility. Further development of a love theme is here prevented because of
the burning social issue. There seems to be no time for
romantic entaglements in the midst of a revolution.

The importance of the social question in this play
is reflected in two others ways. Pablo and Celia, who
are both French, declare their sentiments for the Algerians. Pablo affirms that his heart is with these
"gente de color". Celia had come to this country to
teach, and before long she says, "entre los niños empecé
a amar a este pueblo y a comprender que lo tratábamos
injustamente" (817). In spite of the humanitarian
feelings for the Algerians, Celia deliberately allows
Leo her husband to be caught by the police. She insists
that there was no way of warning him that would not
incriminate other activists. Consequently, the situation
here is one in which the social issue outranks the familial or personal element. This is something which Leo
finds difficult to understand since by nature he is not
an activist.

The relationship between Leo and Celia is by no
means a traditional one. They are a husband and wife
caught up in a revolution. The situation demands that
personal sentiment be sacrificed to the political cause.
Leo's death is inevitable for more than one reason.
First, his kind of marriage cannot possibly last. His
death terminates it. Second, Leo cannot live with his
feelings of shame and guilt for having succumbed under
torture. The sentiment that is most apparent between
Celia and Leo is not the love and total commitment
characteristic of a good marriage. Most apparent are
the pity and compassion which Celia feels for Leo. She
suffers because of his physical pain and more so for
his inability to be a true activist. Celia and Leo do
not meet each other on an equal basis. Celia is more
akin to Pablo than she is to Leo. When Leo enters the
room Celia is more concerned about whether he was followed than she is about his welfare. This does not
mean that no love exists between the two. What we witness is a peculiar Sastrian relationship. In times of

revolution the familial bond becomes subservient to the
social cause. But this is not a requisite for either
personal happiness or revolutionary success. It is a
conflict which is difficult to reconcile. To whom or
to what does one owe one's allegiance first and fore-
most? This conflict Sastre declines to resolve; in one
situation the personal need seems to outweigh the social
and in another the contrary is true. The presentation
of this issue in En la red is one which leaves the spectator dissatisfied. Perhaps Sastre is telling us that
personal sacrifice in the face of revolution is such
that no adequate resolution of the conflict will be
acceptable to all. The curious element here is that
even Pablo accuses Celia of maltreating Leo. Intention-
ally or not, the question that Sastre raises is: what
effect do war and revolution have on human relationships?
Is the correction of social ills worth the grief and
pain that one has to endure? These are some of the
issues raised in the majority of Sastre's dramas for
which no solutions are offered.

Luisa of La mordaza finds herself in a different
situation. She takes the initiative and informs the
police commissioner of the guilt of her father-in-law,
Isaías. It is true that Luisa is the only witness to
Isaías' crime. Yet, when she summons up the courage
to tell Juan, her husband, and Teo, his brother, of
their father's crime, she is made to feel an outcast.
Juan is much too afraid of his father to act like a man
and morally support his wife. He is definitely a coward. The reader is not made to feel that genuine love
exists between Juan and Luisa. The power executed by
Isaías seems to suppress any feeling between husband
and wife. What respect can Luisa feel for Juan? She
sympathizes with his difficult situation but finds the
courage to act and to denounce Isaías. Once the denunciation has been accomplished, a feeling of relief
pervades the home. It has been pointed out that "the
family members suffer from the immediate effects of the
liberating act, but the future holds the promise of a
return to life."[1] It is only natural that Isaías' sons
and Luisa should be saddened at his death. But as Juan
talks of the approaching year and tries not to weep,
one gets the impression that perhaps henceforth he and
Luisa may experience a more solid marraige. Juan tries
to reassure himself and the others: "No lloramos, a fin
de cuentas. Estamos tranquilos. Puede que nos cueste
trabajo confesarlo, pero nos encontramos bien. Hace
buen tiempo. Parece que se prepara un buen año. Si

todo sigue así, el pueblo volverá a resurgir, a pesar
de todas las calamidades. Habrá fiestas como antes.
Las gentes estarán contentas en toda la comarca y nosotros estaremos con ellos, y nos alegraremos con ellos.
Creo que podemos mirar tranquilos al porvenir. Las
cosas van bien, gracias a Dios. No hay motivos para
quejarse, ¿ Verdad que no hay motivo? ¿ Verdad?...". (342).

Interestingly, in spite of the fact that Juan and
Luisa are married, it is the older couple, Isaías and
Antonia, who control the family. When Juan expresses
his sadness he turns to his mother for solace, not to
his wife. It is only when Isaías is dead that Antonia
is no longer subordinate and can function on her own.
Further evidence of Juan's weakness is revealed in
Cuadro III. Luisa has already admitted to the police
that she heard a shot but Isaías has forbidden her to
say anything further. Juan suspects that his wife is
hiding something from him and urges her to tell him.
"Es que si algún día me ocultaras algo, no te podría
perdonar. Es lo único que no te perdonaría. Siempre
te lo he dicho." (310). This seems to be a trite reason for not forgiving one's wife. One could think of
any number of more important issues which would warrant
non-forgiveness. After Luisa tells Juan of his father's
crime, he pleads with her to forgive Isaías. Juan practically insults his wife when he tells her that Teo must
be informed "...Por lo menos, mi hermano Teo tiene que
saberlo. No me sirve que lo sepas tú, porque tú no
eres su hija." (312). Later when Isaías slaps Luisa
for not keeping quiet she calls him a murderer. It is
only at this moment that Teo can tell his father how
much he hates him. Juan is prepared to reject his wife
for the blood bond which unites him to his father. Juan
is so weak with fear that he puts this before his love
for Luisa.

Antonia's situation leads to another role played
by women--that of the suffering, passive wife. Teo
hates his father partly for the way in which he treats
his mother. In addition to the cruelty with which she
is treated by Isaías, Antonia has to suffer the physical
disability of blindness. Indeed, Isaías refers to her
blindness without pity, regarding it as a weakness
rather than a disability.

ISAÍAS.___ Está bien, Antonia... Me gusta que
sueñes... No puedes hacer otra cosa ya..., y hay que
disculparte esas pequeñas debilidades... Pobre Antonia,
¿ cómo has llegado a esto? Ni siquiera puedes vernos

73

claramente... Te mueves entre sombras... No ves más
que unos cuerpos que se mueven a tu alrededor y que
no eres capaz de distinguir..., que te inquietan cuando
tiemblan porque no sabes lo que va a ocurrir y siempre
te parece que va a ocurrir algo malo... (291).

It is Antonia who refers to the heat and to the
crimes that are committed then. The most important
aspect of her life is her belief in God and she prays
for her husband's soul. He is very sardonic in his
expression of thanks to her. A more humble and passive
woman could not exist. As one critic declares, "Antonia
... is humble and obedient and like the people governed
by Gessler, she expects that she will be rewarded for
her passivity. Her religious idealism relieves her of
responsibility to act."[2] Antonia believes only in the
existence of a heavenly justice and this is what concerns her most rather than any earthly social justice.
She discusses this with Jandro her youngest son and
Isaías:

ANTONIA.___ (Niega con la cabeza.) No hay otra
justicia que la de Nuestro Señor Jesucristo.. No debe-
rías olvidarte nunca de ello, hijo mío.

JANDRO.___ Entonces, que habrá que hacer con él?

ISAÍAS.___ Yo te lo diré. Tratar de convertirlo
a la religión. ¿Eh, Antonia? ¿Verdad que es eso? (318)

Antonia asserts that this is her belief but Isaías who
is the very antithesis of all that Antonia represents,
warns Jandro that he should believe otherwise. Antonia
believes in gentility and humility. Isaías advocates
toughness. When Antonia tells Isaías that a person
can only be truly happy in the other world, one sees
exactly how she has accepted with resignation the cruelty of her husband throughout her married life. In
other words, Antonia has not experienced happiness
with Isaías. He, on the other hand, affirms that he
has enjoyed this earthly existence. It is the only
one in which he believes and consequently he feels no
remorse or repentance for any act that he has committed.
The total lack of communication and empathy between
this married couple is also evident in other plays.

In La sangre de Dios, a play which is atypical of
Sastre's theatre, he also portrays an older couple
whose relationship is somewhat reminiscent of that
between Isaías and Antonia. It is a modern day proto-

type of the biblical Abraham-Isaac story. Professor
Jacobo Parthon is convinced that he is receiving messages from God which instruct him to kill his son Ben.
Because of these hallucinations, Parthon becomes completely irrational. Since the death of their other son,
Parthon's wife Laura has not uttered a word. Ben is
convinced that his father did not love his brother as
much as he or his mother did. Since the death of their
son, Laura ceases to believe in the existence of God--
or rather believes him to be a monster if he does exist.
Parthon's peculiar communication with God only serves
to broaden the gap between himself and Laura.

In one of the alternate epilogues of this play
Parthon is convicted of the murder of his son and is
sent to a mental institution. On his release he returns
home and tries to approach Laura. Laura has now regain-
ed her speech. She tells him not to approach her,
denounces him and expresses her disgust of him.

LAURA.___ (Lo ve venir con repugnancia. Lo rechaza
con un gesto.) No, no te acerques. Espero que no te
acerques a mí. Me das asco.

PARTHON.___ Laura... Pero, Laura... Me ha extraña-
do que no fueras a verme nunca. Me figuraba que estabas
más enferma. Pero ahora te encuentro bien. Estás ha-
blando, tienes buen aspecto... Te has curado...

LAURA.___ Me he curado para decirte que me das
asco... (515).

Laura continues by telling Parthon that she has recovered totally. Indeed she declares that it is now impossible for her to suffer or to cry. "Estoy seca y tranquilamente desesperada" (515). Laura confesses to Parthon that she did not speak all those years because she
had nothing to say. Now she does. She despises and
scorns him. It is only after Ben's death that she realises how much she could have said to Ben. Now it is too
late. Laura refuses to accept Parthon's story of his
mystic revelations. She blames everything on his insane
and criminal family and verbally attacks her husband for
having killed Ben. Laura tells Parthon that God does
not exist and curses the day that she ever met him.
She angrily tells him that the only recourse left to
him is to hang himself. Parthon expected that if any-
body could, she would understand. Here the male-female
relationship is the opposite to what we find in La
mordaza. The woman is the one who heaps derision and

scorn on the overly religious husband. Thus, even in
this atypical play, the peculiar, almost loveless, marital relationship exists.

This leads us to the portrayal of love in Sastre's
plays. One critic refers to it as a lack of love and
sees the color grey surrounding everything in Sastre's
theatre--including love. "Con dificultad se puede en-
contrar una escena de ternura de compasión y hasta de
amor entrañablemente sentido."[3] The one play perhaps
in which a feeling of tenderness and compassion does
exist is <u>Guillermo Tell tiene los ojos tristes</u>. These
sentiments exist between Tell and his wife Hedwig.
During Tell's imprisonment he suffers torture and
humiliation. His wife also suffers as much as he. She
endures the mental and emotional torture while her husband suffers the physical. This fact is discussed by
Tell and his father-in-law.

FÜRST.___ Mi hija pensaba que estarían pegándote
y sufría horriblemente. La pobre ha sufrido mucho estos
días. La pobre Hedwig... No sabía qué hacer para con-
solarla...

TELL.___ (<u>Con una voz ronca.</u>) Cuando la he visto
me he asustado un poco. Me parecía que estaba más vieja.
Sí, ha sufrido mucho. Siempre sufre por mí. Podía usted haber casado a su hija con un hombre que no la hi-
ciera sufrir. (614-615).

Although Hedwig remains very much in the background her
presence is often felt through Tell's sentiments. One
gets the impression that Hedwig somehow helps Tell to be
what he is.

Tenderness is evident between Hedwig and Tell as
they talk of their contentment and their lack of reason
for complaint:

TELL.___ Hedwig, querida, no tengo nada que per-
donarte. (<u>Un silencio.</u>) Tú no te das cuenta, Hedwig,
do lo buena que eres.

HEDWIG.___ (<u>Conmovida. Los ojos de TELL están
húmedos.</u>) Tell...

TELL.___ Tú no te das cuenta.

HEDWIG.___ ¿Qué te ocurre, Tell?

TELL.___ Estoy contento. Cuando estoy contento, me lloran los ojos. No es nada.· (<u>Un silencio.</u>) Estoy contento de nuestra vida.

HEDWIG.___ Yo también. Hemos sido muy felices. (635-636).

This scene portrays one of the rare occasions on which any of Sastre's characters express contentment. It is significant though, that Tell's contentment rests with his familial life and not necessarily with his social existence. Not only does Hedwig suffer because of Tell's physical torture but also for her father's humiliation and beatings by the governor's guards. Hedwig feels a premonition of disaster when Tell decides to go out after hearing about Fürst's encounter with the guards. Terrified, she begs Tell not to go but, as if preordained, he tells her that he must. She betrays traditional feminine intuition by sensing the impending calamity. As the play closes and Hedwig attempts to lull Tell to sleep she seems more like a mother figure, attempting to assuage the grief and pain of a son, rather than a wife. In this final scene she succeeds in giving aid and comfort to her grief-stricken husband. Tell thinks that Hedwig should hate him for having killed their son. But instead, she expresses tenderness toward Tell as she endures with him his pain and suffering. Sastre never again depicts such marital sentiment and compassion.

In stark contrast to the Tell-Hedwig relationship, in El pan de todos David Harko and his wife Marta seem unable to operate on the same wave length. As pointed out in the previous chapter, David married Marta (a former prostitute) in an attempt to purify her. Marta's situation in the family is first revealed by Paula, David's aunt. Paula upbraids Marta for being too formal with David's mother and for not acting as if she belonged in the family; but it is evident that Marta feels like an outcast:

PAULA.___ ...Ya sabes que a mi hermana no le gusta que la llames así, señora Juana, como puede llamarla una vecina o cualquier conocida por la calle... Desde que te casaste con David te lo viene diciendo: "¿No soy la madre de David? Y entonces, ¿no eres tú mi hija?" Pero tú no quieres..., te resistes...

MARTA.___ No...

77

PAULA.___ Parece que te empeñas en ser una extraña en la casa, Marta. No sé por qué (233).

Marta continues to discuss with Paula, her relationship with David. She complains that he overworks himself and cannot sleep. He is so engrossed in the cause of the political party that she fears for the future: "Y cada vez lo encuentro más entregado a su trabajo, a la organización de los comités, a la lucha... No sé en qué va a parar todo esto... Yo no me atrevo a decirle nada, pero lo veo consumido, como si estuviera ardiendo por dentro y no se diera cuenta... Y me preocupa..., porque me parece que no podemos contar con él para el futuro ..." (234). Marta's fear is that David is too involved and for this reason will not live to an old age. This fear is ironical, for it is David who terminates his own life by jumping out of a window.

In addition to Marta's concern for David's future, is her expression of the sense of helplessness that she feels since she can do nothing to alleviate David's situation. She is a once fallen woman, now socially redeemed, and evidently David does not consider her sufficiently equal intellectually to understand his political problems. This is what hurts and humiliates Marta most. "Pero lo que me hace más desgraciada es darme cuenta... de que yo no puedo hacer nada por él. Eso me hace sentirme pobre, insignificante... ¿Ni para eso voy a servir? Veo que David se me escapa de las manos y no puedo hacer nada... Veo que no es feliz... Veo que está como enfermo... Entonces, ¿qué hago yo aquí? ¿Por qué estoy en esta casa? ¿Para qué? Usted dice que me empeño en ser una extraña en la casa. ¿Y no lo soy?" (235). Evidently Marta blames David for her feeling as an outcast. Her sense of uselessness is caused by David's refusal or inability to communicate either his ideas or his sentiments to her. As a wife she feels utterly useless and consequently she often reflects on her past life and wonders if perhaps that is where she really belongs. In the life that she led previously she served a useful purpose. Now she feels "yo no puedo hacer nada por nadie" (236). By "nadie" it is obvious that she is referring specifically to her husband. Here it is worth noting that Marta feels more comfortable takling to Paula than either to David or his mother. In fact it is apparent that Marta's purpose in the play is nothing more than to reveal through conversation with Paula, anecdotes about David's childhood and family life. In addition, the fact that

David cannot relate to his wife in any way indicates his concern with political issues rather than with family problems. Marta's concern with the future (even though according to Paula the revolution is over) anticipates the difficult situation which is about to erupt in the familial and political scenes.

After Juana (David's mother) confesses to Paula and Marta that she has accepted money from Pedro Yudd the profiteer, Marta's reaction reveals that her sole concern is for David as a political personality. She tells her mother-in-law that her action has betrayed and isolated David. She seems to know David even better than his mother does. At least she realizes that his reaction and concern will be primarily political and not personal. Marta tells David of her yearning for happy and peaceful family existence. She longs for David to be concerned with personal rather than socio-political issues: "Me gustaría que esta noche pudiéramos estar en paz, charlar tranquilamente por fin. Como si todo fuera bien en el mundo y nosotros nos mereciéramos hablar de nuestras cosas, hacer proyectos para el futuro" (244). Marta is fully aware that David's personal life is dependent on the political situation in the country. This is difficult for her to accept. Marta does not think that she is asking for too much when she expresses the desire for what she considers a "normal" marital existence, but David fails to understand why Marta is unhappy with the prevailing existence.

MARTA.___ ... Pero una mujer, una pobre y egoísta mujer desea tener un marido en casa, un marido admirable que viene cansado del trabajo y, cuando vuelve, abraza a su mujer y se siente satisfecho porque sabe que ha ganado el pan de sus hijos. Un marido que se abandona y se hace como un niño en los brazos de la mujer que es su esposa. Una mujer piensa que no haya nada más hermoso en el mundo y, si es preciso sacrificarlo todo a eso, lo sacrifica. (Tiene los ojos húmedos.)

DAVID.___ No he conseguido hacerte feliz, Marta. Bien sé que no he conseguido nada para ti. He sido torpe. Era fácil hacerte feliz. Tú querías serlo. Pero no contábamos con mi tristeza. No sabes hasta qué punto he deseado tu felicidad. No pedía otra cosa en el mundo. Y estás aquí, en casa, triste, con dos mujeres que tratan de comprenderte. Yo he fracasado. (245).

The irony is that David does not intend to attempt to
ameliorate the situation between himself and Marta.
He expresses his deep love for her but admits that he
has not known how to love her truly. Marta has made
him happy. He has failed to do likewise for her. This
causes him a great deal of sadness; but what causes him
even greater despondency is the failure of the revolution. The fact that hunger persists is the issue with
which David is most concerned. This is the abyss which
keeps these two individuals from achieving togetherness.

David is incapable of seeking a respite from what
he considers to be his responsibilities. The feeling
of emptiness which exists between David and Marta is a
far cry from the close companionship and understanding
which exist between Tell and his wife. There is no
bond which unites David and Marta. The death of Tell's
son brings him closer to his wife. The death of Juana
fails to do the same for David and Marta. When Paula
tells Marta that what David has done to his mother is
unpardonable Marta attempts to defend David. She declares that David has done his duty as a result of
which he is suffering deeply. She tells Paula that he
did not come to say goodbye to his mohter before she
was taken away only because he was afraid of breaking
down completely. Marta seems to accept all of David's
actions unquestioningly. She claims that she was always aware that David was capable of "terrible things".
"Yo sabía que no era un hombre como los demás" (261).
Marta realizes that David would do the same to her if
he considered it politically necessary. Yet she tells
him that she loves him now more than ever. It seems
incredible that Marta could be so self-sacrificing
towards David. She denies that she is disgusted with
his actions. She is so blind and hungry for David's
love that she refuses to feel grieved for what he has
done to his mother. She seems to be nothing without
David. "Estamos en casa. Eso es lo que tienes que
pensar. Yo estoy contenta solo con tenerte entre mis
brazos. Te encuentro desamparado, triste..., y de
pronto yo me siento fuerte junto a ti..., fuerte y
necesaria..., y me doy cuenta de que estoy en esta
casa para algo..., de que no soy un estorbo, una cosa
inútil... La pobre chica que te encontraste una tarde
te quiere..." (266).

Marta's feeling of usefulness is rather short-lived
because David cannot live with himself, in spite of
having Marta's loyalty. In this relationship, Marta

feels herself to be nothing without David and strives
for that bond to unite them but it eludes her. Marta
cannot satisfy David's needs, since those are completely involved with his political commitment. Consequently, her efforts to achieve this unity are futile. She
does not have what David needs to alleviate his situation. Her love is insufficient. He wants to suffer.

MARTA.___ Yo te quiero, David, Te quiero también
por encima de todo límite.

DAVID.___ Y aun contigo, Marta, ¿qué va a ser de
mí?

MARTA.___ No tienes que llorar, David. No tienes
que llorar. (Están abrazados. MARTA le enjuga las
lágrimas.)

DAVID.___ Contigo todo es muy fácil, Marta. Si
hablo contigo, todo se hace fácil. Pero yo necesito
hablar con los que no me quieren tanto, con los que
no están dispuestos a disculpármelo todo. Te necesito
a ti, Marta, y sin ti todo sería muy oscuro, pero también necesito ser castigado. Y para eso estás tú (A
PAULA.) esta noche aquí. Tú, que crees que me merez-
co morir malamente. (271).

Paula now is as necessary to David as is Marta. Furthermore, David needs to know what opinion the people
have of him at this time. Is it horror, pity or
respect? David's torment is too much for Marta's love
and compassion to bear. In fact, her unflinching love
for David seems incredible. If a man can betray his
mother, what can he not do to his wife? Marta's role
as the suffering lonely wife is comprehensible; but
not her role as a totally dedicated mate willing to
suffer under these circumstances. Marta hopes that
finally David has found his peace in death; that he
is now saved; that he can no longer be tormented. His
suicide does not leave Marta with any bitterness. She
accepts even this. Even more unbelievable perhaps is
her simultaneous expression of hope that she will one
day find everlasting love with David. This desire for
unity after death is expressed also in Ana Kleiber.
Thus, the play El pan de todos ends like so many others
on a note of hope; that love and unity which are unat-
tainable in this life might be realized in the life
after death.

La cornada again presents the wife as a victim of

her husband's position in life. Here Gabriela, José
Alba and Marcos form a twisted version of the eternal
triangle. Marcos, the impresario, compels José Alba
to leave his wife and to devote himself totally to the
whims and commands of Marcos. Marcos and Gabriela can
be seen as adversaries fighting for the same prize--
José Alba. It has been suggested that "Alba's need for
Marcos is so compelling that he speaks to him in words
that a lover might use, and Marcos in his dominant role
shows himself to be as intense as José."[4] Gabriela
openly tells Alba how she sees the relationship. "¡Yo
te diré lo que quiere! ¡Lo quiere todo! ¡Quiere que
tú seas suyo! ¡Sí, es eso, suene come suene! Te quiere
como una mujer, más que una mujer, porque no puede ni
pensar que alguien participe de algún modo en tu vida!"
(917). This twisted form of dependency which exists
between Alba and Marcos is what destroys the relationship that exists between Alba and Gabriela.

In the play, even before Gabriela appears on stage
her name is introduced by Marcos. He warns Alba not to
receive his wife if she comes. Alba is afraid to see
her even though, as he says, everything is over between
them. It is obvious that Alba is as malleable with
Gabriela as he is with Marcos. Alba then is the pawn
between the other two. Marcos has complete control
over Alba yet he denies this when confronted by Gabriela.
He insists that Alba is acting independently. Gabriela
is not fooled by Marcos' lies. She confesses that the
only thing that she desires is money. Marcos begs her
to postpone her talk with Alba until after the fight
since he does not want to "play around with José's
life". His gross cynicism is too much for Gabriela.
He even threatens her if she should insist on inter-
fering. In this scene one witnesses the clash of two
dominant characters. But, Gabriela is no match for
Marcos when it concerns José Alba. The latter has
already forsaken his wife in order to follow Marcos
into the bullfighting profession. Gabriela accuses
Marcos of being totally lacking in conscience. Later,
Marcos reveals that he has nothing personal against
Gabriela. He is only opposed to women who will wreck
José Alba's career. He displays his annoyance when
Alicia, a doctor and former friend of José, calls him
up and they agree to see each other after the fight.
Yet when Marcos is unable to help José medically, it
is Alicia who tends his wound. When Marcos is absent
and José needs solace he finds it in Gabriela. Obvious-
ly both these women serve a useful purpose only when
they are needed. Marcos prohibits any other relation-

ship. Marcos tries to assure José that the latter does
not need women.

When Gabriela succeeds in seeing Alba alone, they
both display their need for each other. Gabriela confesses to Alba that she came intending to hurt him,
but instead she falls tearfully into his arms. Alba
too weeps with emotion. It is apparent that he loves
his wife yet he is too weak to stand up to Marcos.
When Gabriela informs Marcos that she and José intend
to go back together, Marcos presents the ultimatum.
José will have to choose between his career and his
wife. Both cannot be accommodated. Alba does as Marcos
bids and tells Gabriela to be quiet. Marcos makes it
plain to both of them that the moment has arrived for
José to choose. He informs them "... Yo necesito a
todo un hombre. No puedo compartirlo con una mujer ni
con nadie... Suena feo, ¿verdad? Pero hay suficientes
historias de mujeres en mi vida para que comprendáis
lo que quiero decir... El toro es así... Hay que echarle
hombres libres y dispuestos a todo... De ahí salen las
figuras. De la paz familiar, ¿qué puede salir? Todo
lo más, algún brillante diplomático... ¡Toreros, no!
¡Ni artistas! ¡Ni nada importante! Eso es otra cosa.
Está hecho de otro barro y es una pena que se pierda."
(918). Marcos is saying that one's career dictates
what kind of life one should live. Gabriela is completely overwhelmed by Marcos and gives in to his demands but not before telling him that he will never
understand her motives. She insinuates that Marcos is
incapable of understanding love. It is because she
loves José that she capitulates for the moment. She
declares her intention of waiting there in the hotel
for José until after the fight. When Gabriela sees
how totally dependent José is on Marcos, she leaves.
She realises that she does not know how to assuage
José's nervousness as he faces the approaching bullfight. She recognizes that Marcos has this ability and
for José's welfare she decides to allow Marcos to have
his way. Gabriela's departure is ironic because it is
exactly at this moment when José desperately needs
Marcos' encouragement and moral support that Marcos
curelly and deliberately withholds them. One critic
states "that Marcos seeks to terrify Alba in order to
regain his dominance. He calmly and cruelly manipulates
Alba's emotions and Alba projects the image of a young
virgin, terrified and fascinated by her seducer."[5]

It appears that as far as Sastre is concerned,
there are times when a wife cannot be of solace to her

husband. A similar situation existed between Marta and
David of El pan de todos. This particular aspect of
"woman's failing" appears as a stereotype in Sastre's
theatre. Perhaps what Sastre is trying to say is that
at some moments in our lives, no other human being can
be of assistance. There are times when we stand completely alone. At these times no other human relationship can suffice. Yet Tell receives comfort from Hedwig
--but David and José Alba are left to endure their torment and fright alone. Marcos succeeds in destroying
the love that existed between José and Gabriela. However, what Marcos seeks as a replacement for this love
eventually destroys the life of two individuals. Clearly, life without any kind of familial love is impossible.
José thinks that he can function without love, but he
is wrong. Unable to cope with the situation, he stabs
himself and eventually dies.

.   In Asalto nocturno the female role is small and
insignificant. There are at least two husband-wife
relationships which are presented but which are of no
great significance. The first is that of Professor
Marcelo Graffi and his wife Mary; then follows that of
Harry and Ana Müller. The latter is the more interesting. Harry is the paid assassin of Marcelo Graffi but
he is presented first in a contented domesticated scene.
He is a murderer who does a job for which he is paid.
Sastre also presents a scene of domestic intimacy between Harry and Ana. The latter is pregnant at the time
that Harry is apprehended. Ana loves Harry deeply and
dislikes the fact that his "work" causes him to be away
from home frequently. Harry, who confesses to Ana that
he has never held any deep sentiments, now wishes that
he can be closer to his wife in her pregnancy. Ana is
the completely passive wife who has no idea of what
type of work her husband is involved in and furthermore
sees no reason to question him about it. She passively
accepts his arrivals and departures. Her lack of curi-
osity reflects a character who is merely a stereotype.
She is not depicted very convincingly. The Graffi and
Bosco women are presented fleetingly. However, the
suffering caused by the men in the families is apparent.
Marga Bosco is presented as the seduced victim of Carlo
Graffi. No relationship exists between the two. It is
a simple case of a man of power exacting his rights as
in the ancient "droit du seigneur". The female victim
is made to suffer a humiliation which eventually forces
her to demand revenge from her brother, because her
father refuses to act. Angelo her brother mentions to

84

Marcelo Graffi that Marga eventually became insane. It
is noteworthy that while the suffering of the women in
the families is only intimated, the revenge of the male
members is a paramount issue.

Tierra roja, Muerte en el barrio and El cubo de la
basura all contain husband-wife relationships. In
Tierra roja the marital alliance is subordinate to the
theme of collective rebellion. Consequently, Sastre
does not depict any significant aspect of married life.
Teresa and Inés are mere stereotypes of the subservient
woman who is always ready to assist her mate. Muerte
en el barrio and El cubo de la basura both present relationships on two levels; namely, that of the young un-
married couple and that of the older parents. In El
cubo de la basura, Germán's love for Julia is utterly
pure. He deliberately keeps this purity intact since
Julia was seduced and abandoned by Pablo. Julia is
from the same pathetic barrio as is Germán. These
people have very little in life with which to be content.
Julia sees in Pablo an opportunity to escape from the
"basura" that is her barrio, and she takes it. When
she contracts tuberculosis Pablo abandons her. On her
return to the barrio, Germán makes no effort to "redeem
her socially" by marriage. Instead he seeks to do this
by killing Pablo. The only important element in Germán's
life is his love for Julia. We are not told whether
his love is ever requited. He actually has nothing to
offer Julia in order to improve her social condition.
Thus, marriage would serve no useful purpose as it does
in El pan de todos. It is "because he is able to give
up his hope for love and personal happiness for a commitment, that he achieves new stature and finds meaning
in his life."[6]

After Julia's return, Germán goes to visit her in
order to tell her that he is leaving the barrio. Julia
thinks that Germán has come to take pleasure in her
misery. She does not comprehend his motives. He expresses his feelings to her "...Te ha endurecido la vida
y no puedes ya pensar que alguien te quiera de verdad
y que sufra con tu dolor y que llore con tus penas. ¿No
te das cuenta? ¿Es que no me conoces? ¿Soy en extraño
para ti? Si de verte sufrir siento que se me rompen
cosas en el pecho y que algo en la garganta me ahoga.
Si pudiera llorar, estaría llorando contigo. Por eso
necesito saberlo todo. ¿Qué ha ocurrido? ¿Te has encontrado sola? ¿Por qué has vuelto?" (123). Germán
is sincere in his declaration and Julia is touched by
this. Julia thinks that perhaps he is leaving the

barrio because she has returned. He does not clarify
his reason for leaving; he merely urges her to try to
forget her sufferings and to get well. Julia's predicament gives Germán some reason for living. He feels
that by rectifying the reason for her suffering he will
demonstrate his utility in life. "... Ayer me sentía
de sobra en el mundo, sí, de sobra..., inservible, como
la más asquerosa basura de una pocilga... Y, sin embargo,
soy un hombre, y es bonito serlo, y ahora estoy alegre."
(125).

Germán confesses that he still loves Julia; yet it
never occurs to him to marry her in order to bring her
happiness. His only thought is to avenge the wrong done
to her. His decision appears illogical since it could
not possibly ameliorate Julia's prevailing situation.
It could only cause her more suffering if Germán is
punished for the crime he commits. In fact Germán's
friends remark on his lack of resentment at the time
when Julia went off with Pablo. Luis maintains that
Germán's only concern is to see others happy. In his
own misguided way he believes that by killing Pablo he
will somehow make Julia happy. After he kills Pablo
he maintains that he now has nothing to forget. He has
now begun to live. The credibility of Germán's actions
and his rationalizations leave much to be desired. His
action serves no useful purpose. It is hardly possible
to believe that he has achieved contentment by murder-
ing Pablo.

Germán's father was killed in the war. Germán's
mother Madre, reflects on the life she had lived with
him as she talks with Señor Tomás, Julia's father.

MADRE.__ (Gravemente.) Mi marido fue un gran
hombre, Tomás. No hay quien pueda decir algo malo de él.

SEÑOR TOMÁS.__ Hombre, claro que no. Era un hombre como hay que ser.

MADRE.__ Sabía tratarme con cariño y al mismo
tiempo sabía mandar en mí. Cuando le daba la gana se
ponía borracho, pero ni eso era un defecto en él. Sabía
hacerse perdonar como un hombre. (148).

Madre ends by cursing the war that took her husband from
her. In her brief description of the relationship that
existed between her and her husband, one can detect the
subservience of the wife to the husband. Madre is the
stereotype of the Sastrian wife; or perhaps she is really

typical of the Spanish wife of her generation.

In Muerte en el barrio, Sastre does not in any way
develop the relationship between Tobías and María,
Juana's parents. In fact the only discernible relationship is their role as parents of a girl who has suffered
deep pain and grief at the loss of her infant child. On
the other hand, a distinct relationship between Juana
and Arturo (the father of her child) is evident. Their
relationship typifies that of the woman abandoned by her
lover. The only thing which kept Juana going was her
child. On his death, she has nothing left. She no
longer has any tangible connection with Arturo. But
the death of the child coincides with Arturo's return
to the barrio; and although Arturo abandoned Juana, he
tells Paco his friend that he will not allow anyone to
speak ill of her or even to criticize him for what he
did to her. When Arturo hears of the child's death
and the fact that the doctor on duty was not at the
clinic he becomes furious. Immediately Arturo's concern
for Juana increases, and one of his friends suggests
that he should go to see Juana. Arturo is doubtful that
Juana would be glad to see him. Juanito his friend
affirms that Juana has never stopped loving Arturo and
this elicits a confession from Arturo that he still
loves Juana. He decides to visit her.

The first time that Arturo visits Juana, at her
father's house, she refuses to see him. When Tobías
realizes that Arturo is truly grieved by the child's
death he confesses that in his heart he always knew
that Arturo had some good in him. Arturo vows to return every day until Juana consents to see him. Furthermore, he swears that he will marry her. Whatever
prompts Arturo's sudden desire for marriage is unclear.
If it is the death of the child, then surely his basis
for marriage is questionable. Sastre, however, does
not elaborate on this theme and provides no further
clue as to whether Arturo will keep his word. The
important issue is not the relationship between Arturo
and Juana but rather the effect of their child's death
on themselves and all concerned. Juana is so distraught
that she walks around disheleved and does not care if
Arturo sees her in this condition. "Quiero que me vea
como estoy, que me vea todo lo fea, todo lo estropeada
que estoy" (558). After all, Juana realizes that she
has nothing to lose. That she may have something to
gain by putting on some makeup does not occur to her.
Juana's preoccupation at this stage is the loss of her
child, winning over Arturo is secondary. When Arturo

87

eventually sees Juana, her complete lack of rancor towards him indicates her priorities. Their conversation clearly illustrates this.

ARTURO.__ (Con una voz ronca.) Juana.

JUANA.__ Hola, Arturo.

ARTURO.__ Juana, no sé cómo decirte, no sé cómo decirte...

JUANA.__ (Sencilla, dulcemente). Has vuelto, Arturo. Creo que te esperaba. Pero tenía miedo de que te hubieras olvidado de mí.

ARTURO.__ ¡Olvidarte, Juana!

JUANA.__ (Mira a ARTURO afectuosamente.) Te miro y me doy cuenta de que me alegra mucho verte, Arturo.

ARTURO.__ ¡Juana! ¿No me guardas rencor?

JUANA.__ (Extrañada.) ¿Rencor?

ARTURO.__ ¡Tenía miedo, tenía miedo de verte!

JUANA.__ (Dulcemente.) ¿Miedo de mí, Arturo?

ARTURO.__ ¡Me he portado muy mal contigo!

JUANA.__ ¿Conmigo, Arturo? Yo no me he dado cuenta. ¿Sabes lo que ha ocurrido? Nuestro hijo ha muerto. ¿No lo sabías? Nuestro hijo ha muerto. Esa es la pobre noticia que te doy al cabo del tiempo. Me hubiera gustado que a tu vuelta nuestro hijo se te hubiera echado al cuello con mucho cariño... Lo estaba preparando para eso, ¡para ti, Arturo! Pero, ¿no sabes, no sabes? ¡Ay Arturo, nuestro hijo ha muerto!

ARTURO.__ (Con lágrimas en los ojos.) Nuestro hijo ha muerto, Juana. ¡Nuestro hijo!

JUANA.__ Me he quedado muy sola, muy solita, Arturo. Tendrás que quererme mucho.

ARTURO.__ ¡Perdóname, Juana! ¡Perdóname! (559).

Ironically it is the death of their child which finally brings these two people together. "Juana feels no need to forgive Arturo since resentment is lost in their mutual loss."[7] It is a typical Sastrian trait that one must sacrifice one thing in order to gain another.

Ana Kleiber is Sastre's only play where the theme portrayed is love; or rather the inability of two people who love each ogher, to find happiness together. The plot, as Sastre tells us, is an amplification of the situation presented in Cargamento de sueños in which a woman deserts her lover for another but eventually returns to the former. In Ana Kleiber, the story is unfolded through a series of flashbacks which tell of the love affair between Ana and Alfredo. At the beginning of the play Ana arrives at a hotel in Barcelona in order to meet with Alfredo Merton after a long separation. She dies of a heart attack before Alfredo arrives. The rest of the play relates the story of these two lovers and the final reason for their proposed meeting at the hotel.

The major theme of the play is the incapacity of two people to find happiness. According to one critic, "el tema principal es el conflicto entre el deseo del hombre para amar y vivir con otro ser humano, por no estar solo, y la naturaleza del hombre que, habiendo adquirido durante su vida ciertos rasgos de carácter y ciertas ideas, le impide llevarse bien con el ser que ama."[8] When Alfredo arrives at the hotel, after learning that Ana has died, he sees his hopes for eternal happiness completely destroyed. He is so distraught that he even considers suicide. The funeral scene reveals Alfredo's grief. He has waited for years in the expectation that he and Ana would eventually find happiness together. Ironically, now it is only in death that he can possess her solely--that no one else can kiss her.

As the story of the lovers unfolds through flashback, Ana and Alfredo meet each other while he is a student in Paris. Their first meeting and their final farewell at her death reflect a somewhat similar situation; for Ana is on the point of committing suicide by throwing herself into the river when Alfredo approaches and offers his assistance. Ana wants to be alone. This is one of her characteristics. Her need for solitude at times often prohibits any lasting togetherness with Alfredo. Ana is a rather libertine young actress and has no qualms about telling Alfredo details of her sordid experiences. As she relates the details to Alfredo, she gets the impression that he is afraid of her. She acknowledges that she possesses some quality

which often frightens men. Alfredo declares that no
man could ever be happy if he truly loved her. Unfortunately this proves to be only too true in Alfredo's
case. Once Alfredo declares his love for her, his
quest for an impossible love begins. Ana warns him that
he should escape while he can but he is already irrevocably drawn to her. She warns him that she "siente
atracción por lo canalla y por lo sucio. Tiene un demonio dentro" (438).

Ana and Alfredo live together for eight days during which he becomes hopelessly entangled with her emotionally. At first they seem happy but then Ana becomes
restless and wants to be alone. She warns Alfredo that
by falling in love with her he has begun the journey
into hell from which he will never escape. Sastre describes Ana's face as being both sweet and diabolical.
This apparent paradox is a reason for the inability of
the lovers to stay together. Ana constantly reveals
contradictory emotions and desires. She feels safe and
secure with Alfredo--yet feels that she must escape
from this security.

After eight days Alfredo returns to his room to
find that Ana has left him. This is only the first
of their painful farewells. In a letter she explains
that she has gone off to join a theatrical company on
a tour of Germany. Alfredo searches for her, finds
her, and discovers that she has been awaiting his
arrival. He resolves to marry her; but Ana's character
will not permit her to be tied down to marriage. That
night the theatrical director enters Ana's room and
after taunting Alfredo about the "good times" that he
has had with Ana, Alfredo kills him. Terrified at his
action, Alfredo realizes that Ana is also disgusted by
his obvious display of fear. He does not report the
murder. Because Alfredo has shown fear and displayed
scorn for theatrical people Ana begins to hold him in
low esteem. She actually taunts him with certain sordid details of her life causing him to flee from her.

During their separation, Ana drinks heavily and
her conduct proves so intolerable that she is fired
from her job. After meeting a third time, Ana and
Alfredo live together. She misses her previous "activities" now that she has become almost a "model house-
wife". During the war, while Alfredo is at the battle-
front, Ana has many encounters with other men. When
Alfredo returns and upbraids her for licentious behavior, she shouts back at him about her need for male

diversion. "Necesitaba entusiasmarme con algo, necesitaba divertirme. Era eso, ¡que necesitaba divertirme! Detrás de la fidelidad no había nada y me di cuenta: ¡solo el vacío y la muerte! ¡El hastío y la tristeza! ¡Y hasta el amor se apagaba en la espantosa paz de todos los días! ¿Quieres saberlo? Para conservar y aumentar mi amor por ti necesitaba sentirme sucia, mancharme..., para que tú volvieras a aparecer en mi memoria como una maravilla que no me merecía, como algo adorable..." (470-471). Ana's complexities now begin to bore Alfredo. He insults her and declares that he can now laugh at himself for having loved her. Ana responds that she needs his insults in order to feel purified. She needs this punishment. Again we find this Sastrian trait of purification through punishment, pain or suffering. Alfredo becomes so angry that he attacks and almost kills Ana. He then returns to the front. After the end of the war, when he returns to Barcelona, he begins to write to Ana. They agree to meet in the hotel. Here the recounting of Ana and Alfredo's torrid love affair ends. In the burial scene, Alfredo refers to the purification of Ana. At her grave he utters "Porque tú, a lo largo de tu vida, no has querido más que a un hombre, a un pobre hombre llamado Alfredo Merton. Es inútil que hayas querido aturdirte y derrumbarte en los abismos. Tú Ana, has vuelto limpia de todo... Te escapabas siempre... Ahora ya te tengo. Has muerto, Ana, y ya no te puedes escapar" (430).

The manner in which the character of Ana is treated bears some resemblance to other female characters in Sastre's dramas. Alfredo's desire to marry Ana, in order to redeem her morally, appears in other plays already discussed. Ana's masochistic attitude, in order to seek moral purification, is presented in a slightly different manner in Escuadra hacia la muerte where the soldiers believe that their punishment will result in a social purification. Ana is the only truly liberated woman in Sastre's theatre--liberated in the sense that although she is dependent on men for her very existence, she chooses not to be subservient to the wishes of her lover! Ana is free to act as she pleases rather than to follow the dictates of anyone. Consequently, she stands apart in her relationship with Alfredo. The relationship most portrayed is that of the dominant male-subservient female. One cannot fault Sastre for this. It is traditional. That perhaps is why Ana Kleiber's depiction is so startlingly different. Even Luisa and Celia, the two women who are able to initiate action and are the dominant members

91

in their marital relationship, do not display the same
sort of freedom as does Ana. In spite of this, Ana is
a most unhappy creature. Men do as she bids. She acts
as she wishes but her search for happiness is unsuccess-
ful. Is there a message here, or is this mere coinci-
dence? Characteristically Sastre provides no answer
to the question. The persistent element here is that
none of Sastre's characters ever achieve complete happiness. Self-sacrifice is always evident.

FOOTNOTES TO CHAPTER IV

[1]Seator, p. 67.

[2]Ibid., p. 66.

[3]Giuliano, p. 212.

[4]Seator, p. 250. See also Anderson, *Alfonso Sastre*, p. 104.

[5]Anderson, *Alfonso Sastre*, p. 104.

[6]Seator, p. 59.

[7]Ibid., p. 212.

[8]Giuliano, p. 202.

CHAPTER V

PARENTAL - FILIAL RELATIONSHIPS

The Sastrian character in addition to being portrayed in a social milieu, is often depicted in a
familial background. The family achieves an importance
in Sastre's dramas which at times is in direct conflict
with social issues. The majority of Sastre's characters, protagonists as well as antagonists, exist within
the parental-filial aspect of the familial milieu. In
certain dramas like El pan de todos the parental-filial
relationship conflicts with the social and political
issue. The family as a whole is depicted in Sastre's
theatre as an important axle around which the various
characters revolve. In some plays the family is merely a kind of refuge for the characters. In others, it
becomes a focal point on the character's life and an
essential element which dictates the behavioral pattern
of the character. In general, the family depicted by
Sastre is the traditional Spanish one in which the
father is a strong, responsible individual who continues to shoulder the responsibility for his children
even though they may be adults and married. Essentially it is the extended family, something which is rapid-
ly disappearing in North American society.

In the traditional Spanish family in rural areas
and small towns, the children who marry continue to
live with their parents and the strong parental-filial
bond is maintained until the death of the parents. The
father continues in the patriarchal role and the children and their spouses are expected to recognize his
role as such and to act in accordance with the patri-
arch's wishes. In the absence of the father, the mother continues to be treated with deference by all and
allegiance to her remains intact. Thus, any daughter-
in-law plays a role which is subordinate to that of
parents. This is the family structure that is portrayed by Sastre. The role of the family as a mere background feature will be examined first.

Prólogo patético as has already been mentioned,
reflects the way in which family ties affect the social
and political issues. Although the chief family concern here is fraternal, Oscar, the protagonist, nevertheless, is in close contact with his mother. In scene
II Oscar returns home and his nervousness is immediately apparent to his mother. His mother attempts to dis-

cuss the political situation with him thereby revealing anecdotes which amplify the political incidents discussed by Oscar and other political activists. Oscar's mother represents the conservative role traditionally assigned to parents. In this case, as happens in many of Sastre's dramas, the mother has experienced grief and suffering because of political and social unrest which her son has not witnessed. She abhors all violence. Her reference to the students' acitivities reflects her desire for peace rather than for further unrest. Her view of the student demonstrations as "cosas de estudiantes [which] esta vez están llegando demasiado lejos" (75), is understandable. Oscar's reply that the students have the support of the workers is countered by his mother who warns him that "los obreros irán por su cuenta, que ni siquiera querrán oír hablar de los estudiantes. Como un día se decidan a matar, empezarán por vosotros" (75). Madre explains to Oscar that her home is her world. She is preoccupied by the fact that something seems to be occurring which neither Oscar nor Julio will discuss with her. They do not wish to worry their mother with political matters knowing that she is preoccupied with her family. The following conversation is indicative of the situation that exists in the family.

MADRE. (Como obsesionada sin oírle.) Tu hermano viene a casa en silencio. Siempre me parece que ha visto "algo" de lo que no quiere hablarme. Siempre trae de la calle un secreto, como una historia inconfesable.

OSCAR. (Sombrío.) Una mujer se ha desmayado de hambre en la calle y se ha roto la cabeza contra el borde de la acerca. Su hija, una niña triste, la mira con los ojos muy abiertos, sin atreverse ni a llorar. Millares de hombres son humillados en cada momento en las oficinas, en los talleres, en los hospitales. Son los siervos de nuestra época. Están acostumbrados a ser humildes, a bajar los ojos, a no tener ningún derecho, a aceptar todo lo que se les da como una limosna. Miran servilmente. No esperan nada. Van muriendo de pulmonía, de abandono, de tuberculosis, de hambre. Eso es lo que ve Julio; eso es lo que no quiere contarte..." (76-77).

When Laura, (Oscar's sister) returns from the movies Madre notices that she too is wearing an expression similar to her brothers. On being questioned, Laura reveals that a bomb explosion has killed many innocent persons. Madre seeks to escape from the violent reality of the situation by sequestering herself at home. Laura's expression of fear that Julio may have been one of the victims causes Madre to scream with terror. Oscar is severe with the women in order to calm them; but they transmit their fear to him. The terror that his mother is experiencing begins to haunt Oscar. Consequently, when the police untruthfully attest that Julio is dead (because of the bomb explosion for which Oscar and other political activists are responsible) Oscar accepts this unquestioningly. The family scene in which Madre voices her terror unwittingly sparks a chain of events which leads finally to Pablo's murder by Oscar. This is Oscar's demise; but now he feels that he has been useful to the revolution and peacefully awaits the arrival of the police.

In El cubo de la basura Sastre presents a family situation in which an adult daughter, Julia, is taken into the loving protection of her parents' home after being abandoned by her lover. Her parents never once reflect any anger or bitterness because of her predicament. Their love for their daughter transcends every other sentiment. When Julia needs her parents they do not fail her. They are prepared to do whatever they can for her well being and happiness. Their selflessness is evident. When Germán asks Señor Tomás, Julia's father, whether she has returned home permanently her father replies, "naturally". He accepts her return unquestioningly. When Germán leaves their home after talking with Julia, she sees the sadness reflected in her father's face. This brief but touching dialogue ensues.

JULIA.__ (Que está sentada de espaldas a su padre y de frente al público. Con voz conmovida.) Padre, yo no quiero que tú estés triste. (Calla, como esperando una respuesta, que no llega.) Si madre y tú estáis tristes, yo no podré vivir. (Breve pausa.)

SEÑOR TOMÁS.__ (Trémulo.) Hija, en esta casa se te quiere. Perdóname... si no he sabido decírtelo... antes... (127).

Similarly, Germán and his mother show their love for each other in an equally brief dialogue. Madre has endured a great deal of anguish throughout many years. She declares that now there is no one and nothing which can make her weep. At this point, Germán declares his deep respect for her.

97

GERMÁN.__ Espero ser digno de ti, madre. De ti he sacado siempre la fuerza para seguir viviendo.

MADRE.__ (Le acaricia.) Lo que no me perdonaré nunca... es haberte traído a un mundo tan triste. Si tú sufres..., eso es lo único que a mí puede hacerme llorar. (146).

Thus, even in these early plays in which the social question is first explored, the deep parental-filial. bond is revealed. This continues to be developed until reaching its fullest portrayal in El pan de todos.

Tierra roja is also set within a family background and in its cyclical character each couple has a daughter. Here Sastre is concerned with the social aspect to such an extent that the parental-filial relationship is not fully explored. In spite of this, the deep bond bet- ween the parents and their daughters is very apparent. As in the case of the wives, the daughters Inés and Teresa are stereotypes and therefore not possessed of any distinctive attributes. In this play the death of a child triggers the revolt of the miners. The mother of the child exhorts the men to begin their attack on the officials of the mining company. She shouts that because they have killed her child there must be blood- shed.

A child's death also serves as the vehicle for seeking revenge in Muerte en el barrio. The death of her child renders Juana unconsolable. "She has lost what she loved most in her life and ephemeral ideas of life that continue beyond physical existence cannot touch her heavy sorrow that is itself a real presence."[1] As she questions the child's whereabouts her mother María responds, attempting to assuage her grief.

MARÍA.__ Todo el mundo sabe que los niños que mue- ren van al cielo.

JUANA.__ No sé... En el cielo... Pero yo he visto su pobre cuerpecito roto; y "eso" que yo quería tanto. que yo besaba y abrazaba, "eso" no está en el cielo, madre.

MARÍA.__ Tienes que tranquilizarte, hija mía.

JUANA.__ Entonces, si eso no está en el cielo, ¿qué es lo que está en el cielo? ¿Qué?

MARIA.__ ¡Yo tampoco lo sé, hija mía! ¡Yo tampoco lo sé!

JUANA.__ ¡Habría que saberlo, madre! ¡Habría que saberlo! (Un pequeño silencio. Sombría.) Es muy importante saber adónde se le va a una un hijo. Yo no me puedo conformar con esas cosas, con que me digan, como por decir algo, "en el cielo"... Yo no sé qué quieren decir con eso, ¡yo no lo sé! (558).

It should be pointed out that Juana who knew her child, is not angered. Rather she is sorrowed and grief-stricken. However, Arturo, the father who never knew the child, is angered and is responsible for the killing of Dr. Sanjo. The mother Juana, plays no direct part in the killing of the doctor. Another aspect of the parent-child relationship is revealed when Juana's parents continue to support their daughter with love and affection even after she has Arturo's child. Her parents are more concerned with seeing after her welfare than in reflecting on any possible disgrace to the family name. Their daughter's happiness is of utmost importance to them.

In Asalto nocturno the utter lack of selfishness is also evidenced in both the Bosco and Graffi families with respect to their children. They are all willing to make sacrifices in order to ensure the happiness of their children. The exception of course is Marco Bosco, who is so afraid of Carlo Graffi that he permits his daughter Marga to be violated by Carlo Graffi. When Angelo Bosco visits Marcelo Graffi, his purpose is to ask forgiveness of the Graffi family in an effort to terminate the feud. His primary concern is the welfare of his son Ugo. The latter has already been shot at and Angelo is prepared to beg that his son's life be spared since he is innocent of any crime. "A mi hijo, en un brazo... Unos días después nos echaban del trabajo, a mi hijo y a mí... ¡Tuve la idea de matarme, de colgarme de un árbol en la calle, para que todos pudieran verme al pasar y se terminara esta historia, y mi pobre hijo pudiera ser feliz algun día! Era un niño cuando pasó, ¿entiende? ¡No tiene la culpa de nada! ¡Que le dejen vivir! ¡Es todo lo que pido!" (761). Flavia, Angelo's wife, exhorts their son Ugo to avenge his father's murder. She makes him look at his father's dead body so that he will remember how he died. This illustrates the family pact that exists between father and son. Tonio Graffi feels that by killing Angelo he has avenged his father's murder. It is as if a debt has to be paid to one's father for the life that he has given for his children.

Escuadra hacia la muerte has only male protagonists. However, the bond which exists between Javier and his mother greatly influences his pattern of behaviour. Javier's father is dead and he laments to Andrés the fact that his father did not live to see his dream realized--his dream that his son Javier would one day be a brilliant and worthy professional (181). After his father's death, Javier's mother becomes the strongest and most important influence in his life. Consequently, the letter which he writes in his diary is dedicated to his mother. In it he confesses his cowardice and terminates the letter as follows... "En el momento en que voy a firmar esta declaración, pienso en mi madre. Sé que ella estará despierta y llorando... De eso sí que nadie puede consolarme en el mundo... Nadie puede enjugar de mis ojos... el llanto de mi madre..." (185). Thus, his only concern is for his mother.

While on guard duty, Javier is deeply introspective and is overcome by his seemingly hopeless situation. The cold weather only intensifies his feeling of frustration and fear. In this state of mind he calls on his mother for aid and comfort: "Yo no quiero caer prisionero. ¡No! ¡Prisionero, no! ¡Morir! ¡Yo prefiero... (Con un sollozo sordo.) ¡morir! ¡Madre! ¡Madre! ¡Estoy aquí..., lejos! ¿No me oyes? ¡Madre! ¡Tengo miedo! ¡Estoy solo! ¡Estoy en un bosque, muy lejos! ¡Somos seis, madre! ¡Estamos... solos..., solos ... solos...!"(191). "As a way back to his innocence Javier longs to return to his childhood and his mother's love. For him she represents unconditional love and absolute safety, someone whose concern and protection are a shield from the world."[2] Javier seeks to reach out to his mother but she is a mere fantasy. The love that he needs is unavailable from any one of the condemned squad. The only love he has known is his mother's. Consequently, in his isolation, solitude and the cold weather he seeks the only source of warmth that he knows. One critic, Lynette Seator, maintains that Goban here seems to be the father image; and since Javier does not win any love from this authoritative figure, he seeks to escape into these fantasies of his mother.[3] She also sees a contrasting type of relationship here in the severe unquestioning type of father image of Goban and the soft tender love of the mother. One may also observe here a God as a father image that unrelentingly exacts payment for crimes committed. The element of fate seems to be linked with this God image. Although this idea is not expressly voiced by Javier, nevertheless, the impression transmitted is that they are being punished like children by an authoritative figure, first evidenced in Goban and later in a God-like type of figure. This unknown being is punishing them for the "mysterious and horrible sin" which is supposed to have been committed. The parent-children relationship here is vague but reflects some bewildered misguided children being punished by an unrelenting and severe parent figure.

La mordaza also contains the relationship of a severe father, Isaías, as a God-image type of the Old Testament; one who shows himself to be completely authoritarian and demanding and ready to inflict punishment for any crimes or sins committed. The children, (all adults), Juan, Teo and Jandro fear their father more than they love him. The fact that he is their father implies that these sons are expected to love Isaías; yet, by his very nature and his repulsive commanding attitude towards them, he undermines any deep feelings of love and causes sentiments other than love to awaken in his sons. As Leonard Pronko points out love is not necessary in Isaías' estimation since he counts on the effectiveness of fear as a gag.[4]

From the first scene of the play we see Isaías as a commanding, self-centered individual who expects complete obedience and deference from his family, particularly the children. Antonia, Isaías' wife, is concerned about Teo's apparent preoccupation. Isaías, however, is irritated that Teo has dared to absent himself from dinner. That, he says, is his only concern. When Antonia attempts to continue her train of thought, Isaías orders her to shut up, adding that any attempt to excuse Teo is repugnant to him. "Calla. Me repugna que todavía trates de disculparlo. Lo que hace con nosotros no tiene perdón. Estamos aquí todos reunidos a la mesa. Es un desprecio que hace a la familia" (289). At this point, Luisa, the daughter-in-law, is the only one who dares to suggest that she sees no affront in Teo's absence. This irritates Isaías, who indicates that it is no business of hers and that it is his concern solely. He continues adding insult to injury, "y si lo que te molesta es mi modo de ser, podías haberte evitado el fastidio de sufrirme. Bastaba con que no hubieras entrado a formar parte de esta familia que, por lo visto, te desagrada tanto" (290). Luisa finds the courage to retort that only Juan is her family and

that she refuses to be ordered by Isaías. This infuri-
ates Isaías even further and he tells Juan that he is
no man to allow his father to be insulted in this fashion. He threatens that if Juan is unable to subdue
Luisa that he himself will do it. Luisa reacts with
spirit to this threat which causes Isaías to openly
criticize Juan's choice of a wife. After shouting that
Luisa is probably possessed by the devil he adds, "Tiene
cien gatos dentro del cuerpo. Es una pena que no tuvi-
eras más ojo para elegir a tu mujer, Juan. El mundo
está lleno de mujeres honestas, limpias y obedientes"
(290). At this juncture Juan finally summons enough
courage to humbly request that his father desist from
such allegations and that he is happy with the choice
that he has made. This only makes Isaías more angry
and he now decides to direct his fury towards Juan by
attempting to degrade him as a man and as a son. "Tú
eres un muchacho de muy poco talento, Juan. De pequeño
llegaste a preocuparnos a tu madre y a mí. Eras como
un animalillo torpe. El médico nos dijo que la culpa
de todo la tenían tus nervios. No tenías memoria y
hablabas con dificultad..., te costaba trabajo... No
sabes la tristeza que nos dio tener un hijo así. ¿verdad,
Antonia? Nuestro primer hijo. Nos dio muchà tristeza"
(290). This crushes any courage that Juan may have
felt and he ashamedly begs his father not to relate any
more such accounts of his debility. Isaías counters
further stating the great disappointment that Juan has
been as a son.

Isaías and Antonia reveal in their discussion what
their expectations as parents are and what they were.
These vary greatly as can be expected since Antonia
being the submissive wife that she is has been interested only in loving and being loved by her children.
She is content merely because she has been a mother.
and furthermore she is happy with her children as they
are. She is grateful just to have them near and love
her. Isaiás rejects this statement by Antonia while
he hurls pity and contempt at his wife for being so
"soft" with her children. As each person attempts to
defend the other Isaías chooses that person on whom
to hurl his scorn and derision. Thus, Luisa, Juan
and Antonia all find themselves at the receiving end
of Isaías' insults for merely attempting to state their
own opinion which happens to be contrary to what Isaías
holds. Isaías terminates this scene of the family's
support of one another against him by blaspheming them
all as being utterly useless creatures. His sarcasm
is boundless as he concludes, "es un poco triste mi

situación rodeado de todos vosotros, débiles y enfermos.
El más viejo tiene aún que daros lecciones de fuerza y
de coraje... (Añade, amargamente.) Una pandilla de
inservibles, eso es lo que le ha tocado en suerte al
viejo Isaías Krappo para consuelo de sus últimos años
... (Sonríe irónicamente.) Una pandilla por la que
siente un gran amor, a pesar de todo..." (292).

The only member of the family who is exempt from
Isaías' sarcasm and wrath is Jandro, the youngest son.
The father tells Antonia that he is convinced that
Jandro is the only one who possesses any voluntad.
Yet Jandro is the only one who does not take part in
the discussion and who therefore fails to come to the
defense of any of the others. Isaías is pleased with
the hard work which Jandro does in the fields and tells
him complacently that some day he will be grateful to
his father for having made him work in this fashion.
It appears that Isaías expects total obedience from
his children and this he finds only in Jandro. The
irony of the situation is that this is what Isaías
sees as will power. Yet any independent thought or
action on the part of the others is seen as unforgiva-
ble insubordination by Isaías.

Teo's return that night sparks further anger in
Isaías. Teo stayed out late only to prove his independence to his friends. The following conversation
indicates the sentiment of father to son and the desperate desire of Teo to indicate that he is not afraid
of his father.

TEO.__ Hemos estado... en la taberna. Hemos
tomado unos vasos de vino. Hemos estado cantando. Yo
quería venirme ya, pero me decían que me quedara. Me
gastaban bromas. "¿Tienes miedo de que te riña tu
padre?", me decían. Y yo me he quedado con ellos para
que vieran... (LUISA vuelve. Va junto a Juan que,
inquieto, lía un cigarrillo, y le pasa una mano por el
hombro. Observan la escena.)

ISAÍAS.__ ¿Para que vieran qué?

TEO.__ Para que vieran que yo soy un hombre y que
no me asusto por cualquier cosa. Así que me he quedado
y hemos estado divirtiéndonos un poco. Pero yo estaba
deseando venirme, padre.

ISAÍAS.__ Estábamos todos sentados a la mesa; la
familia reunida para la cena, como debe ser... Hasta

te hemos esperado un poco... Queríamos estar todos
juntos, como siempre... Sabes la importancia que tiene
para nosotros esto... Lo sabes porque ésa es la educa-
ción que te he dado...Pero tú, a esa hora que es sagra-
da para nosotros, estabas en la taberna emborrachándote
... Es triste.

TEO.__ Padre, yo no quería ofenderos tanto.

ISAÍAS.__ (Sus ojos relampaguean.) ¡Eso es lo
malo! Que no querías ofendernos. ¡Eso es lo malo!
Que hacéis las peores cosas sin querer. Si lo que hubieras querido es ofendernos y lo hubieras hecho por fas-
tidiarnos, para que nos diéramos cuenta de tu desprecio,
sería otra cosa... Esto sería una lucha y no una repri-
menda paternal... Sabríamos a qué atenernos..., las
cosas estarían claras... Pero estas situaciones son
ridículas... Vete, vete a dormir. Déjame en paz. No
quiero ni verte. Me da asco que seáis así. (294-295).

Teo's fear of his father is, however, very apparent.
This has been a feeble attempt to prove his manhood. The
fact that Teo reiterates that he did want to come home
is indicative of the fact that he indeed has no will
power and that his actions are subordinate to his
father's wishes. Isaías reminds Teo, in a manner reminiscent of a strict and overbearing parent, of the
family custom of dining together. As far as Isaías is
concerned this external type of family togetherness
(that is, the physical aspect) is important, even though
he may be aware of a lack of spiritual togetherness.
The family ritual is of great importance to Isaías.
He is insulted that at the ritual of the family dinner
which he considers sacred, that Teo was imbibing. The
irony is that Isaías does not believe in God and that
he ridicules his wife Antonia for what he considers an
idiosyncracy. In spite of this he talks about something being sacred to him. It is obvious here that
Isaías is the God of the household and he therefore
establishes the particular importance with which any
event or action is to be considered. In fact, he is
outraged that Teo did not intend to offend the family.
He would prefer it this way, for this would indicate
a positive decision on Teo's part and would result in
a good family struggle, which Isaías would relish.
Instead, he is faced by a futile attempt at insubordination which produces derision on his part. He therefore does not even consider it worthwhile to involve
himself in a verbal fight with Teo. Teo's action apparently does not merit his anger. He sees it merely as

a thing to be ridiculed and he does exactly this. His
final words to Teo to go to bed and leave him in peace,
suggest the attitude of a parent who is bored by the
childish antics of his son and who merely wants to be
left alone. Teo's inability to counteract his father's
attitude and words further indicates that he is as
spineless as his father suggests and that Teo's action
is childish and should be dismissed as being unimpor-
tant.

A further scene between Isaías and Luisa reflects
the hostility which the latter fees towards her father-
in-law. He asks for her respect and friendship but she
counters this with a blunt statement that she finds him
disagreeable. He attempts to excuse his apparent insults to her by indicating his affection; but Luisa
rejects his overtures declaring that she feels a great
aversion for him. Isaías continues with a rather in-
sincere attempt to win her affection stating that he
accepted her from the beginning as a friend and that it
is obvious that she has been influenced by rumors concerning him. Luisa denies that she has ever listened
to gossip. Her father-in-law then attempts to reach
her physically--something which she repels. Fortunate-
ly for Luisa, at this moment Juan appears; but not
before Isaías has revealed his physical desire for her.
This incestuous desire places Isaías even further in
an unsympathetic light. Luisa's rejection of his advances enhances her own position and character. Fur-
themore, Isaías' lack of guilt (or even lack of awareness of his misconduct) also indicates that his morals
differ from those of his sons and daughter-in-law.

When Luisa is a witness to Isaías' shooting of
the forastero she goes into a state of shock and acqui-
esces without protest to his command to be silent.
Previously, she showed that she was not afraid to resist him. Now she does not resist. One possible explanation is the fact that he actually threatens her
with death. During the investigation Isaías denies
to the police commissioner that he or any one else in
the household heard a shot the previous night. When
questioned, however, Luisa admits that she did hear it.
Isaías feigns surprise while he upbraids Luisa for her
admission. After the departure of the police, Isaías
admits to Luisa that the murdered man did come to the
house; but he warns her not to admit anything to anyone
--particularly not to Juan. He tries to make Luisa
believe that his action was committed for the preser-
vation of the family. In effect Isaías tries to make

Luisa an accomplice. In his attempt to persuade Luisa
to do his bidding, Isaías alludes to Juan's great love
for him and actually employs this as a device to ensure
silence. This seems to work temporarily. Luisa maintains her silence for two reasons: first, her life has
been threatened and she fears that Isaías is capable of
effecting his threat; and secondly, she knows how deeply Juan will be hurt by her accusation of his father as
the assassin. She cannot bear the thought of hurting
her husband. In his own way Juan does love his father
and is acutely affected when he discovers the truth.
The result of this "gag" on Luisa is that she is left
in a condition of extreme nervous tension.

After Juan learns of his father's guilt from Luisa,
he feels that he must unburden himself by informing Teo.
Juan tells Luisa that her story is incredible. He knows
that his father killed during the war but insists that
Isaías is no assassin. He acknowledges that Isaías has
a disagreeable nature: "Tiene mal carácter; todo lo que
tú quieras. Pero no es un criminal" (311). Luisa
agrees with Juan and attempts to explain Isaías' actions
by enunciating her belief that he must have been provoked to such action. Juan goes even further by suggesting that his father must have suffered temporary in-
sanity. When Luisa repeats Isaías' contention that his
life had been threatened, Juan seizes on this idea like
a man who is desperately seeking a satisfactory explanation. Consequently, he immediately insists that his
father be forgiven.

JUAN.__ Entonces es que tuvo miedo. Tuvo un enorme
miedo y lo mató para defenderse del miedo... En un momento de locura. Hay que perdonárselo. Yo se lo per-
dono a mi padre. Para mí no es un criminal. ¿Y para
ti, Luisa? (LUISA guarda silencio.) Hacía calor--mi
madre siempre lo dice: que los días de calor son malos
....--y mi padre estaba nervioso...¿Tú qué piensas?
(LUISA guarda silencio.) Ya veo que tú no se lo vas a
perdonar, Luisa. ¡Y sin embargo, hay que perdonarle,
hay que perdonárselo todo a mi padre! Es muy viejo y
tenemos que ser buenos con él en estos momentos. (312).
Juan's desperate attempt to vindicate his father's
action seems to spring more from compassion than from
love. He is appealing to Luisa because of his father's
age. This a pathetic plea which only serves to indicate
that there is nothing in Isaías' character which his
son can honestly uphold as a means of justifying his
action. Yet Juan intends to maintain his loyalty to
his father. When Luisa points out that the stranger was

shot in the back in cold blood, there is no defense
left for Juan. He feels that this burden must be shared
at least by Teo, because Juan's character is such that
he is not sufficiently strong to shoulder this responsibility alone. Luisa reiterates Isaías' threat to her,
if she should disclose anything, but Juan is adamant
that Teo must be told and that his father would not dare
carry out his threat to Luisa.

Juan is startled by Teo's complete lack of surprise
at his disclosure of their father's guilt. Teo, however, informs Juan that several companions of the victim had informed him of the man's identity and of his
reason for coming to their house that night. When Teo
relates calmly the atrocities committed by Isaías
against the victim's wife and daughter during the war,
Juan appears stupefied. He is the eldest son but it
is obvious that his fear of his father has prevented
him from admitting honestly to himself exactly what
kind of character his father really is. It should be
pointed out that Teo is fully aware of Isaías' wartime
folly and for this reason is readily able to believe
his father's guilt. The following dialogue indicates
the different sentiments which the two sons have for
their father.

> TEO.__ ¿Tú no sabías que el padre había hecho...
> algunos horrores durante la guerra?
>
> JUAN.__ Nosotros no lo veíamos durante meses, y
> nadie se atrevía a contarnos nada.
>
> TEO.__ Pues ese es nuestro padre; una especie de
> demonio que nos atormenta. (Un silencio.)
>
> JUAN.__ Tú no quieres nada al padre, ¿verdad?
>
> TEO.__ No.
>
> JUAN.__ ¿Le odias?
>
> TEO.__ (Con una mirada vidriosa.) Creo que sí.
> (314).

As Juan naively questions Teo's feelings of hate, the
latter mentions several reasons for his sentiment.
His father's cruel treatment of their mother, his humiliation of her, and his ridicule of Teo before Julia,
a girl whom he loved, have hardened any feeling of
compassion that he may have felt. Indeed, Teo tells

107

both Juan and Luisa: "Sé que es un pecado, pero odio a mi padre con todo mi corazón." (315). Nevertheless, Teo is not prepared to denounce his father. He admits that it is not love but fear that prevents his doing this. His father causes him to "tremble like a woman". In fact he has no doubt that if Isaías were to suspect that Teo might denounce him Isaías would kill him. Thus, in Juan we see compassion for his father rather than love, and complete naiveté regarding his father's character. In Teo we see both fear and hate with the former outweighing the latter and thus influencing his attitude towards his father.

Jandro is not cognizant of his father's guilt. Yet he is outraged at the act for which his father is responsible and angrily reveals to his father and mother his sentiment concerning the culprit. He would advocate, if he could, that the culprit be hanged in the square as an example. Furthermore, Jandro would prohibit his interment in sacred ground and would relegate the burial to "... un camino, para que todos pisaran en su tumba y no tuviera un momento de descanso" (317). Isaías does not seem bothered in the least way by his son's views. In fact he prefers to torment Antonia cruelly because she would advocate pity and forgiveness for the culprit.

In a subsequent scene Isaías taunts all his children, including Luisa, who informs him that the police are about to apprehend the culprit who has been identified by a witness. Isaías is seemingly aware of what some of them know, yet he criticizes them all for being nervous and slow in their work. Juan admits to his father that it is all too much for him. Teo, on the other hand, nervously admits to feeling unwell and is afraid that God will punish them all. Isaías cruelly taunts Teo on hearing this statement until Teo begs his father not to be blasphemous and to admit to the existence of God. Luisa comes to Teo's defense as Isaías torments him and confesses that she has told his sons that their father is the murderer. The reactions of the family are varied. Jandro bursts into tears, Antonia is stupefied and Isaías, enraged, slaps Luisa. Juan feebly tells his father to leave Luisa alone but the latter courageously screams that Isaías is a murderer and is perfectly capable of killing her. Even at this moment Juan does not want to believe this and begs Luisa not to say it. Teo, now incapable of maintaining his silence, shouts that what Luisa says is the truth. At this moment he releases all his pent-

up emotions and tells his father exactly how he feels:
"...Padre, vas a oírlo de una vez. Vas a oír lo que
nunca te he dicho. Hoy he tenido tanto miedo, que ya
no siento nada. Vas a escucharme. Te odio. Eso es lo
que quería decirte. Pero no te odio desde ahora. Te
odio desde antes de que mataras a ese pobre hombre. Mi
odio no tiene nada que ver con tu crimen. Te odiaría
tanto aunque no hubiera ocurrido nada, aunque estuviéra-
mos aquí tranquilos, cenando, y yo te mirara, como siempre, con timidez y tuviera el mismo miedo de siempre...
Te odio..." (322). No one responds as Isaías forlornly
asks whether they are going to desert a poor old man
who is alone.

Two months pass by, and autumn arrives, and still
the family keeps the information to themselves. Teo is
of the opinion that they may maintain their silence forever. He would like to break the silence but fear of
his father prevents him. Luisa keeps silent solely
because of her love for Juan. She is no longer afraid
of Isaías. Juan and Luisa discuss his parents during
this period. According to Luisa, Antonia weeps only
because Isaías will not confess. She is concerned with
his eternal condemnation rather than with the crime per
se. Juan, still shocked into apparent disbelief,
attempts to analyze his father: "A mi padre la vida le
es suficiente... para vivir... Nosotros necesitamos de
otras cosas que están más allá..., de los misterios del
catecismo..., de creer en cosas que no vemos... Porque,
si no, la vida sería para nosotros demasiado amarga...
Pero mi padre es tan fuerte que no necesita de nada...
Cuando se muera, no habrá nada en el mundo que él no
haya hecho..., ni un solo placer que no conozca, ni
una emoción, ni una vergüenza... El habrá pasado por
todo... Lo habrá gozado y sufrido todo... (324).

Although Isaías is ailing during this period, he
gets out of bed to accuse Teo, Juan and Luisa of plot-
ting against him. Furthermore, he says that he got out
of bed because he knows that they cannot manage the
affairs of the house without him. He questions how
they will fare when he is dead. This illustrates that
Isaías has never given his sons, (adults though they
are) an opportunity to look after his affairs. Consequently, he does not think them capable of handling
matters. When Juan suggests that his father return to
bed, he becomes irate and in order to prove his strength
challenges any of them to a fight. On Juan's suggestion
that the fever is affecting Isaías, the latter upbraids
him for daring to raise his voice and threatens to hit

him. Isaías will never concede that his sons are adults.
He insists on treating them as if they were boys who are
to be physically manhandled in order to control their
behaviour. Isaías, consequently, threatens to kill
them all when he is in better health. He defies them
to tell the police anything. He is counting on their
fear since he knows that he cannot count on their love.
Yet he dares to warn them that they will be eternally
sorry if they were to reveal anything to the police.
"... No os tengo miedo. Veo que estáis todos contra
mí. Pues no me importa. Os desafío. No diréis nada
a la Policía porque no sois capaces. Sería demasiado
terrible para vosotros. Ya veo que no puedo contar con
vuestro cariño.. No me queréis. Contaré con vuestro
miedo. No me importa. Los muchachos guardarán silencio, ¿verdad? (Ríe burlonamente.) Si alguno llegara a
hablar se arrepentiría. Os lo juro. Y los demás no
podrían perdonárselo nunca. Ninguno de vosotros podría
ser ya feliz. También os lo juro..." (328). Thus,
even as his health and strength fade, Isaías, continues
his effort to impose the gag of fear on the entire family.

Finally Luisa is unable to bear the burden of
silence any more and sends for the police commissioner.
She admits to him that she was a witness to the crime
and that everyone in the family now knows of Isaías'
guilt. However, Luisa is still terrified that Isaías
will kill her and that no one will come to her defense.
The commissioner assumes that Juan will protect his
wife. Luisa, however, tells him otherwise: "Usted no
conoce a esos hombres, señor comisario. No se atreve-
rían a defenderme. Tienen horror al viejo. Le tienen
horror." (333). Even at this moment Luisa has no con-
fidence in her husband's ability to defend her against
his father. After the commissioner leaves he orders a
policeman to guard Isaías. The latter, in the policeman's presence, forcefully embraces Luisa as he attempts to squeeze from her some admission of affection.
When Luisa screams to be set free the policeman inter-
venes and brutally subjugates Isaías. In the epilogue,
the family attempts to come to grips with the situation
after Isaías' incarceration. Luisa regrets having
talked to the police since Juan no longer speaks to
her. She is thinking of leaving the household. Teo,
however, tries to assuage Luisa's fears concerning
Juan and suggests that she should not leave the home.
He tells her that Juan will soon realize exactly what
kind of man their father really was, and that he des-
pised them all. Teo, unlike Juan, feels no grief.

He is now free to come and go as he pleases without any fear of being tormented. For this reason, he is glad that his father has been imprisoned. Jandro, on the other hand, thinks differently. He says that regardless of what his father has done, he still deserves their respect as children. Consequently, he cannot and will not forgive Luisa. The three different attitudes of the sons bear noting. Juan seems to be in the middle path, bewildered by it all and not knowing what position to take towards his father or Luisa. Teo is adamant regarding his father's atrocities and his disdain for the children and is glad that Isaías has met justice. He therefore feels that Luisa acted rightly. Jandro, the youngest, naively suggests that filial respect be taken to its extreme and that Luisa should be considered unpardonable. These three attitudes, vary but they all reflect the way in which Isaías treated his sons and the emotions that he aroused in them. Hate and fear in Teo, a forced love in Juan, and blind respect in Jandro.

In order to bring Juan to his senses, Luisa finally tells him of his father's advances towards her. Once more he is incredulous even though he realizes that Luisa is telling the truth. Finally, when the news of Isaías' death is received, the emotions elicted are varied. Jandro weeps but Teo urges him to stop for as he knows Isaías has deliberately chosen this way to die (shot while attempting to escape) in order to take revenge on the family. He reminds them of their father's promise that they will never be happy. He tells them all that Isaías did this "para dejarnos ese recuerdo; para que nos horrorizáramos, y tú, Juan, tu pusieras tan pálido como estás ahora. Para que Jandro se echara a llorar con ese desconsuelo. Para eso se dejó matar" (341). Juan as usual is bewildered and unsure about accepting Teo's rationalization. Yet, emotionally he is willing to accept it since it would make everything much easier to endure. At this moment Juan feels at peace, no longer bewildered and tormented. But he is sad; and unable to make up his mind, he turns, weeping, to his mother. Juan has not been able to cut himself away from the apron strings of his parents, even though he is the eldest and married. Consequently, Antonia, the half-blind aged mother, has to step in and take control. They all feel more at ease as she exhorts them to go on living and working while she prays for Isaías' salvation. Thus, throughout this play, the parents have relegated their adult children to a subservient role in which all their actions are questioned and they are expected to be subject to their parents' wishes.

The parents here, particularly the father, are the nucleus of the family around which every member rotates.

In Guillermo Tell tiene los ojos tristes, the relationship between Tell and his son Walty deserves to be mentioned. Tell first talks about Walty when he tells his father-in-law Fürst that he cannot stay to participate in the meeting since Walty is ill. Walty is Tell's first preoccupation. He is a sickly lad who is loved by both parents. Tell's wife and son are of utmost concern to him. This is one case in which the family situation outweighs the social. Consequently, Tell's tragedy is the more difficult to bear because it is his son whom he loses. This creates a deep internal fury which ultimately propels him to kill the governor. Tell speaks of the great love which unites him and Hedwig to their son. "Hedwig, tenemos un hijo que nos agradece la vida que le hemos dado. Hedwig, ¡si tú supieras! Hay hijos que miran a sus padres con odio porque los han traído a la vida. Hay muchachos que dicen: '¡Yo no quería!', o que gritan: '¿Quién me ha pedido permiso para nacer?', o también: '¡Yo no os dije que me trajerais, padres!' Los padres de esos muchachos están tristes. ¡Y a veces son chicos fuertes, sanos, que no han estado enfermos nunca! ¿Tú no sabes? Hay chicos que se suicidan y nadie sabe por qué. Los padres de esos muchachos tienen motivos para estar tristes. Nosotros, no, Hedwig. Nosotros muy contentos, ¿verdad?" (635). It should be noted that neither Tell nor Hedwig takes their son or his love for granted. They do not demand anything from him the way that Isaías does from his sons. For this reason, Tell and Hedwig receive their son's love with gratitude and are content with their lives. After Gessler informs Tell that he is to shoot the apple which will be placed on Walty's head, Tell and his son feel their loneliness as no one dares to come to their assistance. This further emphasizes the deep bond that exists between father and son. Walty urges his father not to weep for him. He is content with the life that he has known and is not afraid of the consequences. He tries to assuage his father's fear by assuring him that he will be successful. If he fails then it is God's will. After Walty's death, Tell refuses to have anything more to do with his country politically. He asks to be left in peace. He and Hedwig have lost what was dearest to them because no one dared to aid them. The play ends with Tell and Hedwig in their solitary grief attempting to continue with their lives as best as they can. As Hedwig suggests, perhaps they can find some reason to continue

living. Nevertheless, their lives can never be the
same without the wonderful contentment that they and
Walty found in each other.

The parental-filial relationship reaches its cul-
mination in El pan de todos. This plot is based on the
myth of Orestes in which the protagonist sacrifices the
life of his mother. Giuliano suggests that although
this play is well developed, the theme is perhaps too
horrific for the public.[5] This same critic declares
further that "David Harko representa... al hombre dis-
puesto a hacer el máximo sacrificio por la revolución.
Como hombre del partido pudo denunciar a su madre, pero
como ser humano su propio acto le dio asco y no pudo
seguir, sólo le quedaba el suicidio."[6] Consequently,
this clash between the human and the political being
is inevitable. Another critic, Lynette Seator, suggests that although the man of politics gives the appearance of strength, in his denunciation of his mother
as an enemy of the party, this is a facade.[7] In fact,
it can be taken as a sign of weakness that David is
unable to permit his love for his mother to supersede
that of his dedication to the party. David feels "the
necessity to prove himself through his fanatical act
of party loyalty."[8] David orders a purification of
the party since the people are still suffering for lack
of bread and other important items. Juana, David's
mother, as has been pointed out,[9] is one of these people. Yet he permits his mother to be detained and shot.
Leonard Pronko views David as one who is fighting for
ideas rather than for people. He should therefore be
condemned since his revolution becomes personal.[10]

Juana's appearance from the beginning is that of
a physically and emotionally tired individual. She
has suffered greatly for her family and the revolution
has done nothing to ease her burden. Even though David
is an adult with a wife, his mother still feels responsible for him. It is largely on his account that she
becomes involved with Pedro Yudd. It is her son's welfare which motivates Juana. She does not take the
money for purely personal gains or selfish satisfaction.
She wants a better life for David. It is obvious that
Juana considers the revolution a failure. In spite of
David's involvement with the party, his mother still
goes ahead making her own plans for his survival as
if he were still dependent on her. She is typical of
the mother who refuses to let go, who continues to act
as if she were still responsible for her offspring.
Juana, however, refuses to admit to David that this is

the case. She tries to make him believe that her moti-
vation is purely selfish; and that she did not commit
the crime because of him. "Lo hice porque soy egoísta;
porque no podía resignarme a la miseria en que vivimos,
porque estamos trabajando todos en la casa, y aun así
tenemos para malcomer. Lo hice porque tú no lo hacías
mientras las demás lo estaban haciendo" (256-257).
Once Juana realizes that David is committed to the party
and that he is going to sacrifice her for the cause,
she begs him not to suffer on her behalf. She tells
him that she is ready to die. Her concern is all for
her son as she pleads:

> ... Yo quisiera que tú no sufrieras por mí. A mí
> me gusta terminar. Estoy más cansada de lo que tú
> supones. A mí me gustaría morir. Si es eso lo
> que te apena, el que a mí pueda pasarme algo, no
> debes preocuparte. Yo me encuentro de sobra.
> Para mí la vida no es algo que merece la pena.
> He vivido mucho y estoy harta. Deseo estar en paz
> por fin..., estar muerta... ¡Oh! Veo que vas a
> sufrir, a pesar de todo... Veo que vas a sentir
> terribles angustias... No podré perdonármelo...
> ¿Sabes? Me gustaría no haberme hecho querer por
> ti... Haberte hecho llorar de pequeño. Haber sido
> mala contigo siempre. ¿Sabes para qué? Para que
> ahora no fuera para ti tan doloroso lo que se
> avecina ..., para que esta noche pudieras dormir
> ... Pero en lugar de eso, no he sido más que una
> madre buena y torpe... una madre estúpida... (258).

Juana wishes that David would not feel love for her,
for this is what is making him suffer. If he could
feel some resentment towards her for something she may
have done to him it would make this burden easier for
him.

As it is, David's deep love for his mother gets in
the way of his ideals. This conflict results in the
apparent triumph of the political and social question
over the familial. However, his suicide questions
this triumph, for it is obvious that his love for his
mother proves to be too deep for the issue to be resolved so easily. Paula, David's aunt, considers his
act unpardonable. When his wife Marta comes to his
defense with the excuse that David said he could not
do anything to save his mother, Paula counters that one
can always do something to save one's mother--even if
it means committing a crime. Marta replies that David
does not think this way. His way of thinking is con-

trary to his mother's. She would make any sacrifice for
her son but he allows the party to stand in the way of
his commitment to his mother. The conflict which arises
in David proves that he is not wholly governed by party
ideology. It is not too late to save his mother but
David continues to suffer rather than try to extricate
her from her fate. What is more, he wants to suffer.
He knows that he deserves this and for this reason he
welcomes Paula's presence. She will never let him forget what he has done. She tells him bitterly that
he will not die easily. She foresees that he will eventually be driven to suicide. The fact that Juana refused to speak to David on his last visit to her causes
him great torment. Any words at all would have been
preferable to silence. He refers to his mother in his
long monologue to Paula, "Yo quería que me dijera algo,
pero ella no tenía nada que decir, o no se atrevía a
decirlo... Va a morir sin que yo sepa lo último que ha
pensado, sin que yo sepa cuál ha sido su dolor más
profundo, para que yo no pueda sufrirlo, para que yo no
pueda torturarme con él." (272). Paula, however, does
not let David off easily. She condemns him bitterly as
she tells him of his probable acclaim as a hero. His
fellow comrades will respect and admire him for what
he has done. This is what David wants, but Paula tells
him he will serve not only as a model for party dedication but also as a fearful example to many mothers:
"¡Servirás de ejemplo a unas juventudes malditas, y
desde ahora todas las madres mirarán a sus hijos de otra
forma! ¡Porque desde ahora las mujeres tendrán miedo
de sus hijos! ¡Contigo empieza un nuevo tiempo, David!
Un tiempo en el que todo estará permitido! ¡No eres
feliz pensándolo?" (274). David finally begs Paula to
be silent. He cannot endure the torture any longer.
He confesses that he is not strong as he or others
thought him to be: "¡Yo no soy fuerte! ¡Ahora veo que
no lo soy! ¡He ido más allá de mis propias fuerzas!
¡Todo el mundo ha confiado demasiado en mí! ¡Han puesto
en mí sus esperanzas! ¡Pero no sirvo! ¡Pertenezco
todavía al mundo en que tú vives! ¡Estoy aquí, aterro-
rizado! ¡Tiemblo! ¡Quisiera pararlo todo, destruir el
patíbulo! ¡Perdón, camaradas; yo os pido perdón! ..."
(275). At this point David has begun to crack under
the strain. His suicide is moments away.

The relationship between David and Juana is indicative of the type in which a deep love exists between
mother and son. The mother and son, however, differ in
their particular goal in life. Juana wants all that is
materially and spiritually good for her son. David has

his country's interest as his prime concern. His love for his mother is forced into the background by political and social ideology. Hence, their reaction to Juana's position differs. Juana is resigned to her imminent death. She, an individual, is no match for the collective body--in this case the revolutionary party. David's emotions force him to view her death with horror. His emotions finally overcome him--this man of ideas. Consequently, the ideal mother-son relationship is disrupted because of social and political issues and ideology.

Although La sangre de Dios lies outside the mainstream of Sastre's theatre, it nevertheless warrants discussion in this chapter since a father-son relationship which would otherwise have been obscure is highlighted. One has to remember constantly that this play is based on the Abraham-Isaac story in which the characteristics of the Old Testament God are related in a version in which the God is presumed to be the Christian God. This portrayal stimulated many of the objections raised against this play. In the story, one has two relationships to consider, 1) Professor Jacobo Parthon and his son Ben, and 2) God the Father image against Jacobo Parthon. In other plays Sastre has questioned the existence and the nature of God. Here, this is done explicitly but not with any distinct bias since Sastre has written two versions of the denouement. In the first, Jacobo explicitly obeys the commands of a seemingly inhuman and cruel God, and kills his son Ben. In the second, the assassination of Ben is aborted by the screaming of Ben's fiancée, Sofía. Parthon uses the knife to kill the dog which attacks Sofía. In the first version the cruelty of God prevails as He commands his spiritual son Parthon to kill his biological son Ben. In the second, the love of the Christian God triumphs since the dog becomes the sacrificial lamb. In addition to the opposing views of God as a father image, presented in the two versions, conflicting images are presented by the views of Parthon and of his former student Luis Opuls. According to one source, "Parthon says that God suffers with the suffering of his creatures. Luis, however, sees God as something quite different, something alien, strange, unknown, immobile, cold...unchanging...fixed, serene, quiet, invisible, unconcerned."[11] Laura, Parthon's wife shares this view. In her suffering, after her elder son's death, she screams that God does not exist and that if he does exist he is a monster. She goes further by saying that "Si de verdad hubiera

un infierno, allí estaríamos los que hemos sufrido tanto
que no hemos tenido más remedio que gritar, los que hemos protestado, los que hemos sido injustamente tratados
y no hemos podido soportarlo, ¡los inocentes!" (520).
Sastre continues this controversy over God's nature,
through the personages of Parthon and Laura, without
resolving it. Consequently, the relationship between
God the father and man his son turns out to be one in
which man reveres or disbelieves in God depending on
the particular view he holds of God's nature. Man's
faith is the key to the relationship.

The Parthon-Ben relationship is more clearly delineated. The Parthon family home inspires fear in Ben.
He cannot forget that his insane grandfather killed a
man in the house. Now his father has been fired from
the University for his peculiar mystical aberrations.
Ben tells Opuls that his father seems very strange at
times; yet he loves and respects him deeply. Ben's
mother Laura has not spoken since the death of Ben's
brother and Ben tells Opuls that he fears that his
father did not love his brother as much as he or his
mother did. Ben is forced to think this way because of
the seeming indifference and religious indulgences of
his father. Parthon talks to Ben about God's command
that he kill Ben as Abraham almost did to Isaac. As
a prelude to this, Parthon tells Ben how much he loves
him. Ben in turn confesses his profound love for his
father. This is something which in real life might
seldom occur between parent and child. The love
is usually taken for granted. Parthon tells Ben that
a father and son should speak to each other in this
fashion at least once in their lifetime but this is in
fact an unusual occurrence. Perhaps the necessity for
this declaration of one's feelings is not always apparent. In this case it is Parthon who instigates it and
he does so knowing that he intends to kill his son in
order to prove his faith in God, his spiritual father.
This is incongruous and perhaps is a reason for the
apparent failure of this play. Even the alternate denouement does not save this play since the previous
presentation of God's cruelty and Ben's love are irre-
concilable. The parent-child relationship here is
false and even the God-Parthon one is artificial.

Considering the parental-filial relationships
presented by Sastre, it is clear that he is concerned
with presenting the traditional Spanish family, full of
love but at times characterized by an authoritarian
father and an often acquiescent mother. Frequently,

the mother is forced to intervene on behalf of her offspring in opposition to the overly authoritarian father.
In this type of family, as presented in La mordaza, the
father's love for his children is obscured by a demanding, selfish attitude. The children are either fearful or hateful of their father. The mother's love is
evident but obscured by the father's less than ideal
relationship with the children. In other plays such as
Guillermo Tell tiene los ojos tristes, the love between
the parents and their child is deep. It demonstrates a
positive mutual awareness and gratitude for their good
fortune. El cubo de la basura and Muerte en el barrio
contain relationships between parents and their daughter
(who has suffered the indignity of an unhappy love affair) and reflect the daughter's dependence on her parents' love and understanding as well as the unfailing
support which the parents show to their offspring. All
of these relationships, varied though they may be, demonstrate the strength and viability of the family as
it exists within the social milieu.

FOOTNOTES TO CHAPTER V

[1] Seator, pp. 178-179.

[2] _Ibid._, p. 156.

[3] _Ibid._, p. 157.

[4] "The 'Revolutionary Theatre' of Alfonso Sastre", p. 115.

[5] Giuliano, p. 180.

[6] _Ibid._

[7] Seator, p. 30.

[8] _Ibid._, p. 31.

[9] Van der Naald, p. 44.

[10] "The 'Revolutionary Theatre' of Alfonso Sastre".
p. 116.

[11] Farris Anderson, _Alfonso Sastre_, p. 81.

CONCLUSION

The family in the plays of Alfonso Sastre reflects the same structure as that of the society. In both the family and society, Sastre often presents the tyrannical figure versus the oppressed. Therefore it is not surprising to find a parallel type of reaction from the oppressed in both the familial and social milieu. In addition, conflict at times arises in the individual who is confronted with the choice between family and society and the power and influence which the one may exert on the other. It has already been demonstrated that the family is a viable and sustaining force in Sastrian dramas. Yet it has been stated that "its positive and integrating force cannot extend far enough to shelter and protect a man throughout his life. He must contend with the cruelties of the outside world and care about other people as well as those he loves as family members if he is to become a mature and responsible being."[1] The individual therefore cannot exist solely in the familial world; though his ability to survive in a hostile society depends on the strength of family assistance. There are individuals who do not have this family sustenance and who find themselves struggling to exist in an alien world. These individuals are hopelessly pitted against society and their lack of, or rejection of, family bonds renders them inadequate to cope in the social milieu. The Sastrian character cannot stand alone. He is unable to bear the anguish and pain which results from his conflict with society. Society as seen in Sastre's plays is harsh and cruel. Those who manage to survive their anguish always have a loved one to whom they can turn for comfort.

A classic example of this situation is seen in the plight of Guillermo Tell. Tell's concern for his wife and son outweighs his social preoccupation. He protests the atrocities committed in the name of Gessler and is beaten and incarcerated for a week. On his release, Tell informs his father-in-law Fürst that it is all over for him now. He is now "frío con furia", (615) and refuses to take part in any more protests. He tells Fürst: "Estoy harto. Quiero volver a casa, a mi trabajo. Quiero estar en paz" (616). Tell fully intends to commit himself totally to his family; but the humiliation which Fürst suffers at the hands of Gessler's soldiers, and his resulting suicide, motivate Tell to action. Had his family not been involved, Tell would

not have found himself in that particular predicament.
Gessler further compounds the issue by involving Tell's
son Walty. Since Tell has to shoot the arrow through
the apple that is placed on Walty's head, his self-
control is tested to the very limit. It is no surprise
that in Sastre's play, the protagonist loses his son
to society's evil whims. Gessler is a product of society and his tyrannical rule is exemplary of a cruel
society. Tell has to struggle, not merely against
Gessler, but also against the society which he represents. After Walty's death Tell turns to his wife
Hedwig for solace. Tell will be unable to continue
living if Hedwig does not forgive him for killing their
son. Thus, it is the family strength which permits
Tell to endure life which Gessler, as the representa-
tive of society, had made almost impossible. The tranquility which Tell desires is not possible; at least
not for a man regarded as his country's hero. It seems
that in Sastre's theatre, family tranquility and happiness are incompatible with active social participation.

Escuadra hacia la muerte provides another example
of the close family unit shattered by a cruel society.
The war separates Javier from his mother--the only person who is able to give him the necessary strength and
solace to withstand society's ills. Without her,
Javier is led to commit suicide since he cannot endure
the isolation brought about by being one of the condemned squad. Pedro also is a victim of society and its
cruelties. The rape of his wife by enemy soldiers is
what propels him to commit atrocities upon prisoners
of war. The fact that he no longer has any familial
bonds causes Pedro to go almost berserk, to yearn for
death, and finally to come to the decision to turn himself in; for he has no one for whom to live. Consequently, although none of the characters' family appears
on stage, the effect and influence of the family in
these two plays is of utmost importance when considering the actions that these two men finally take. Here
the family is subordinate to society and in fact is
no match for the social struggles in which Pedro and
Javier become involved.

Muerte en el barrio and El cubo de la basura are
further instances where the warmth of family affection
enables the individual to cope with the harsh realities
that society presents. In El cubo de la basura Julia's
parents offer her the warmth of their home, and their
love and devotion, when she returns to the barrio after
being deserted by her lover. The fact that Julia con-

tracts tuberculosis results in her being treated by
Pablo as if she had a social disease. Julia's illness
causes her to be rejected by others in society. For-
tunately, the family bonds remain intact and Julia is
able to function in society once more because of the
love offered by her parents. Germán's killing of Pablo
is not strictly a familial issue. It is personal; and
from Germán's perspective the social order is subordinate to personal concern. Nevertheless, Germán is
still governed by rules of society; and in the end,
when the police arrive to apprehend him, the social
issue clearly outweighs the personal.

In <u>Muerte en el barrio</u>, Luis the consumptive
patient is pitted against society. Unfortunately, he
has no family ties to console him and has to accept the
affection of Genoveva, the nurse in order to survive.
Juana, on the other hand, has the devoted love of her
parents. It is they who love and support her after
she is deserted by Arturo. Juana's love and devotion
for her son also help to sustain her. On his death
she feels bereft. It is at this moment that Sastre
reveals the care and deep affection which Juana's parents feel for her. The loss of her son is attributed
directly to society, for Dr. Sanjo is little more than
a reflection of the harsh realities of society. His
carelessness and disaffection for his work as a physi-
cian illustrate the defects in society. Dr. Sanjo is
not portrayed in any familial background and appears
isolated in his struggle for survival in a situation
which he detests. He is forced to continue practicing
medicine in order to maintain a livelihood until
Arturo and his friends, themselves a reflection of
another aspect of society, terminate his life. Arturo
and friends are forced to take justice into their own
hands since society does not provide them with adequate
ammunition to satisfy their needs. They are victims
of society since their struggle to exist is hampered
by their low social status. Dr. Sanjo, who represents
a higher level in society, also becomes its victim.
In this play everyone loses the struggle against society since the societal framework is too powerful and
restrictive to permit individual lifestyles. The very
song which the guitarist sings in the bar is indicative
of the people's desire for a better life:

> Ansiosos de vivir
> una vida mejor
> llegamos a este Centro una mañana...
> (575).

123

Tierra roja portrays a happy united family which has to contend with the cruelties of society as represented by the mining company. The little-improved lot of the miners over the years represents a portrait of actual society. The family unit helps to give some purpose to life. Without it, the individual would be lacking. It should be pointed out that Pablo's reason for coming to work at the mines is the same which Pedro had some years previously. This is revealed through a conversation between Inés and Pablo:

INÉS.__ ¿Por qué no se ha quedado en la ciudad? Es lo mejor que podía haber hecho.

PABLO.__ No podía quedarme. He tenido que venir aquí.

INÉS.__ ¿No encontró otro remedio?

PABLO.__ Tenía que irme de allí.

INÉS.__ Habrá otros trabajos... en otros sitios...

PABLO.__ No hay. He venido aquí cuando ya lo había intentado todo.

INÉS.__ Entonces todo sigue igual.

PABLO.__¿Qué quiere decir?

INÉS.__ Que todo sigue igual que hace muchos años ... Mi padre también dice que cuando llegó a las minas ya lo había intentado todo. (352).

Not only has there been no improvement for the working man, but he also has little opportunity to move from the mines to something better. Inés says as much to Pablo when she comments further that the miners have had to accustom themselves to life in the mines since they have always been unable to extricate themselves and to find something better. She echoes the total lack of faith in society when she tells Pablo, "No tengo ninguna esperanza. La vida me ha enseñado a no tener esperanza." (353).

Pablo who is new to the mining life can still express positive emotions such as fury and anger. He is still able to put up a struggle against the confines on his existence established by society. The others however, are no longer able to struggle against society's

harsh realities. It is for this reason that Pablo
tells Inés, "Es que yo no soy todavía un resignado.Usted
está acostumbrada a ver la cara de los resignados...,
la triste y fea cara de los resignados." (355). It is
with a great deal of effort that Pablo succeeds in removing the resignation of these men and in inciting
them to riot. Pablo gives credit to women and the
fact that they are able to carve a home for their families from the hard rock that is society. This family
haven is man's only solace against the outside world.
Pablo expresses it in these words: "Gracias a ellas
las familias salen adelante, los hijos se crían y los
hombres encuentran que su mísera choza es un hogar..."
(356-357). Soceity, however, triumphs over the individual when the striking miners are dispersed by the
authorities. The social struggle of the miners is
pitiful. It is no match for the societal framework
of the mining company. At the end, even when Joven
declares that the situation has improved somewhat, the
impact which society holds over these men does not
decrease. Their resignation is only slightly allevia-
ted. The social struggle will go on. This is one's
lot in life. Society will always be a demanding and
at times tyrannical, force with which we will have
to contend.

The idea that the peacefulness and contentment of
the family man is incompatible with a heroic figure is
also reflected in La cornada. José Alba, unlike Tell,
has no family to sustain him. Marcos, Alba's manager,
implies this when he tells Gabriela, Alba's wife, that
he needs a whole man as a bullfighter, not one who can
be distracted by family concerns: "... Yo no puedo
hacer nada solo con un poco... Yo necesito a todo un
hombre. No puedo compartirlo con una mujer ni con
nadie... Suena feo, ¿verdad? Pero hay suficientes
historias de mujeres en mi vida para que comprendáis
lo que quiero decir... El toro es así... Hay que echarle hombres libres y dispuestos a todo... De ahí salen
las figuras. De la paz familiar, ¿qué puede salir?
Todo lo más, algún brillante diplomático... ¡Toreros,
no! ¡Ni artistas! ¡Ni nada importante! Eso es otra
cosa. Está hecho de otro barro y es una pena que se
pierda." (918). It is economics, one aspect of social
life, which forces Alba to abandon his wife and studies
for the glory of bullfighting. He finally succumbs to
his fears and to the ordeal of fighting because Marcos
chooses to withdraw his moral support. Since Gabriela
has been rejected by José Alba in favor of Marcos, Alba
now has no family from whom he can seek solace. Marcos

thinks that he has given Alba affection but it has not
substituted for true familial affection. Now, when he
needs that family support in order to face the ordeal
that awaits him in the outside world, he has no one
who can give it to him. Society, in the form of Marcos,
has disrupted the family unit. Consequently, Alba cannot cope with what society expects of him. His public
career is over and with that, Alba unintentionally destroys himself. One can see in Platero's plea (the
former bullfighter) at the end for alms, just how difficult the struggle for survival is in this cruel world.

Oficio de tinieblas does not revolve around a family unit. The very lack of a family's presence is
felt by Ismene. She is now a prostitute and ironically
was introduced to her "profession" by her mother, who
died penniless and without friends. Consequently, at
the age of sixteen, Ismene is forced to battle her way
through life as best she can without having the warmth
and sustenance of a family to protect and guide her.
She is thrust into, and left to the mercy of, cruel
society as represented by Vanel and his friends. Vanel,
(as Ismene relates it to Miguel) is the one who machinegunned a hospital complete with patients while he was
in North Africa. Miguel, without a family, has no one
whom he can trust when he learns of his predicament.
Vanel represents that cruel society with which Miguel
is unable to cope. Neither Miguel nor Ismene can find
the warmth of family love which they both need and
desire, for survival. Miguel loses the struggle when
he is killed by Vanel.

In La mordaza, the family structure represents
society with its tyrannical ruler--the father Isaías
and his subordinate children and wife. In this play
Luisa is forced to denounce her father-in-law as being
a murderer. The fact that she has to break family
bonds in order to do this poses serious consequences
for Luisa. She has to endure the almost complete with-
drawal of her husband's love and the wrath of Jandro,
her brother-in-law. Yet Juan's mother Antonia does
not attempt to victimize Luisa for her action. Even
though Luisa's intention is to bring social justice to
bear, the threat against the family unit makes the issue
a tragic one. Isaías attempts, through his death, to
penalize the family forever; to instill guilt complexes
in them that they will never be able to truly function
as a family without suffering some remorse. Here we
have a situation that is typical in Sastre's plays.
The struggle for social justice involves family self-

sacrifice; but even though social justice seems to triumph, one is left with the feeling that victory is incomplete. The family will never be truly tranquil and in their lives will never achieve that personal contentment for which every human being strives.

So far we have witnessed the happy family unit in conflict with a harsh society, or suffering the lack of any family solidarity, thus resulting in the triumph of social injustice. Another aspect of this question which can be explored is that in which family and society seem to be pitted against one another in such a way as to cause a very deep mutual struggle. The plays which best reflect this are <u>Prólogo</u> <u>patético</u>, <u>En</u> <u>la</u> <u>red</u>, and <u>El</u> <u>pan</u> <u>de</u> <u>todos</u>. In the first of these plays, it has already been shown how the struggle to maintain the family unit intact is threatened by the desire for social justice. In this instance, Oscar is duped by the police inspector into believing erroneously that his brother is killed in a bomb explosion which he caused. This is the same policeman who tells Oscar that the only thing that truly concerns him is his own family. During Oscar's incarceration, physical and mental torture begin to affect him. At this moment he yearns for all the members of his family: "¡No sé lo que ha occurrido! ¡No sé lo que he hecho! ¡No sé dónde está mi hermano! ¡No sé qué hace mi madre! ¡Me siento aquí como una criatura desamparada sin noticias de fuera!... ¡Sin mensajes, sin noticias!... Solo..., sin saber nada..., en esta celda horrible. No hay derecho a tener a un hombre en una celda así... Un hombre necesita ver caras de hombres... Ver cómo alguien compra un periódico...¡Porque si no, puede volverse loco! ... Un hombre, por muchas cosas horribles que haya hecho, tiene derecho a hablar con su madre... Es lo único que no le pueden quitar, aunque haya matado a un niño a golpes..., ¡aunque sea un envenenador... o un incendiario!... Un hombre tiene derecho a eso para asegurarse de que en su casa van a dormir... y de que allí están todos menos él..." (85-86). As Seator states, "in an alienated world, the home remains the focal point of existence where the individual is sustained by love."[2] Oscar can endure the torture, but he is unable to bear separation from the family that he loves and which means everything to him. It is for this same reason that Oscar is calm when he is apprehended at home by the police. He mistakenly murdered Pablo since he blamed him for Julio's supposed death. On realizing that Julio is unharmed he recognizes the importance of social justice and is prepared to accept any punishment for this crime. His acceptance is made all the more easy since he has the assurance that all the members of his family are safe. In this play, Sastre gives all the characters a social awareness. For the inspector and Oscar, however, the family is the focal point of their existence. In spite of this, the inspector is required to perform duties which are totally involved with social justice. Consequently, he assures that his family remains intact and totally removed from his work. Oscar, on the other hand, because of his commitment to the revolution is from the beginning irrevocably implicated in the social struggle. However, his allegiance to his family interferes with his total-commitment to the cause and detracts from it. This is a situation in which Oscar's struggle to be loyal to the cause and to his family simultaneously is equalized. Oscar's family remains intact while concomitantly he achieves his desire to suffer for the social struggle.

En la red is the classic example of the social struggle paramount and almost completely eclipsing the familial struggle. Sastre seems to be telling us that family love cannot protect the individual from the cruelties of society as long as social injustice prevails. This is made absolutely clear in the presentation that Sastre makes of the activists' isolation and total preoccupation for the cause. The Algerian couple Tayeb and Aïescha have allowed their political dedication to virtually annihilate any deep mutual expressions of love. Yet one does feel that they are truly in love and deeply care for each other. The same can be said of Celia and Leo, although the case is stated more implicitly. Leo the thinker has joined his wife in the struggle to liberate the Algerians. However, he cannot comprehend Celia's conviction that the social struggle is of more importance than their marital relationship. But this is indeed the case. Celia is so immersed in political intrigue and opposition to what she considers to be the social injustice meted out to the Algerians, that she places Leo's life and safety in second place. The fact, too, that no relationship is permitted to develop between Celia and Pablo indicates the emphasis placed on the social cause. Sastre does not hesitate in this play to show which issue is the most important. Yet this very triumph of the social over the familial leaves the reader with a feeling of dissatisfaction. The sacrifice is too great and the price placed on the triumph of the social and political cause seems too high. In this instance, the dedication to the social issue is such that the warmth and shelter of the family unit is not needed--at least not by Celia

128

and Pablo. One may surmise, however, that the lack of
this very entity deprives Leo of the mental and physical
endurance that is necessary. Further, one may conclude
that in Sastre's theatre the sustenance of the family
is necessary for the withstanding of social struggle--
but Celia and Pablo prove to be exceptions. Their being
handcuffed together at the end may be taken as an indication that, even if they could withstand the lack of
the family protection, they would still need personal
interdependence.

El pan de todos presents the ultimate situation in
the struggle between social issues and one's family.
The sacrifice of David Harko's mother for the sake of
the revolution is too much even for David to bear. He
commits suicide. One has to agree here with Sastre that
it would be too much if dedication to the social and
political cause results in the sacrifice of a parent's
life. The reader would not come away merely dissatisfied but angry. David's suicide atones in some way for
the betrayal of his mother, yet one cannot forgive him.
He has committed the ultimate betrayal. The fact that
Sastre presents the inner torment which David is forced
to endure before his suicide is a reflection in Sastre's
theatre of the family remaining a focal point in everyone's existence. Familial ties are not to be denied
because of the very nature of the social framework
within which one is forced to live. The statement which
has been made in reference to Tell can be applied to
all of Sastre's theatre. "Alfonso Sastre nos está afirmando siempre que necesitamos establecer un equilibrio,
una solidaridad, una communión en el seno de la existencia humana, entre la vida social y la privada. Tenemos que evitar esta alienación a que está sometido el
hombre, que no la resuelven las revoluciones políticas
o sociales, aunque la revolución sea su primer paso."[3]
David's aunt Paula represents the voice of the family
as she verbally chastizes David for his act. One can
empathize with her in her feelings of disgust and yet
compassion for David. She truly holds him in pity for
she senses that he has alienated himself from his family, and from society, and that he will never be able
to live with himself. She predicts his suicide. Clearly in this context, political and social dedication cannot be permitted to take precedence over family devotion.
Such is contrary to the laws of nature. One must feel
for his family first and then for society as an extension of these sentiments. (It is for this reason that
David's act inspires horror in his fellow-revolutiona-
ries as well.) David's neglect of his wife further

underlines his error in judgment by placing the revolution before her and her needs. Afterwards, he looks to her for solace but it is too late for them to truly relate to each other in the manner she had desired. Paula's words are more powerful than Marta's for Paula underlines the fact that the horror that she feels at David's act will be communicated to the people. The alienation that David now feels is similar to Tell's when he did not receive public support. In both cases, family members are sacrificed to the social cause although the circumstances are vastly different. Tell, however, has Hedwig's love and comfort as always. David never needed Marta before, so now her attempt at solace does not suffice.

Throughout Sastre's theatre, one finds the protagonist or antagonist influenced by some family background. For the most part the family extends love and security to the individual, which the latter needs in order to combat the cold and hostile nature of the particular society. The individual is usually placed in a circumstance which demands some sort of personal sacrifice in order to ameliorate the social conditions. This sacrifice often involves the family. Consequently, family understanding and love is a prerequisite for existence in one's society. Without this, the alienation and attendant difficulties which the individual suffers are paramount. However, if family warmth and sustenance is available and welcomed, the character succeeds in enduring the harsh realities represented by society. One cannot, however (like Tell), choose to isolate oneself in one's home, away from society. Society is an extension of the family and man has to accept the responsibility which society demands in order to enjoy a complete existence. Hence, social and familial struggles exist side by side and the individual has to utilize the strength offered by the family in order to combat the struggles presented by society. The one never completely effaces the other. Both the family and society are of supreme importance in our everyday existence.

The official censorship which existed at the time proved to be a source of frustration in that many a stage production was prohibited or curtailed after a few performances. Yet, Sastre continued his dramatic output. The many plays authored by him serve as a testimony to this. In addition, censorship was instrumental in curtailing the activities of the Theatre Groups that were formed from time to time. Obviously, censorship also created financial problems for the Theatre Groups and further hampered any possible productions. The fact that Sastre participated in the polemic with Buero Vallejo concerning the "posibilismo o imposibilismo" of drama was directly related to the problems he had to face regarding censorship. This polemic enabled him to openly criticize the type of censorship that was being exercised in Spain. The legitamacy and inconsistency of the censorship was the source of greatest concern and although in 1963 a censorship committee was formed, the same type of criticism could be leveled at it.

Official censorship has been practically abolished now and although many of the restriction applied to the theatre during the Franco regime no longer exist, it is the consensus of many who attend the theatre that the theatre in Spain has still not recovered from the rigid censorship previously enforced. The present state of the theatre still reflects the need for further training of actors and for further development in theatrical expertise. Still, in the years to come the Spanish theatre without the constraints imposed by censorship with respect to publication and performance, should prove to be a viable and vital form of entertainment once more. However, Sastre may have to overcome any diverse public opinion concerning the alleged involvement of his wife Genoneva Forest in the Carrera Blanco assassination and the subsequent imprisonment of both his wife and himself in 1975. It is to be hoped that Sastre will continue his dramatic output presenting plays that are not only intellectually, socially and politically viable but also dramatically worthwhile.

FOOTNOTES TO CONCLUSION

[1]Seator, p. 11.

[2]Ibid., p. 234.

[3]Pérez Minik, "Se trata de Alfonso Sastre...", p. 26.

BIBLIOGRAPHY

Primary Sources

Plays by Alfonso Sastre

Teatro, Ed. José Monleón. Madrid: Ediciones Taurus, 1964. This edition includes valuable essays by drama critics on Sastre, articles by Sastre, a bibliography and "Documents" on the Spanish Theatre by Sastre and José María de Quinto. The three plays included are Cargamento de sueños, Prólogo patético and Asalto nocturno.

Obras completas. 1. Madrid: Aguilar, 1967. All of Sastre's original published plays are included in this collection except for the Arte Nuevo group and the two done in collaboration with Medardo Fraile. A valuable preface by Domingo Pérez Minik is also included. Each play contains prefaces with pertinent remarks by Sastre.

Escuadra hacia la muerte. ed. Anthony M. Pasquariello. New York: Appleton-Century-Crofts, 1967.

La mordaza. ed. Isabel Magaña Schevill and José Luis S. Ponce de León. New York: Appleton-Century-Crofts, 1972.

Muerte en el barrio. ed. Robert L. Bowbeer and Gladys I. Scheri. New York: Harcourt Brace Jovanovich, Inc., 1973.

Books and Articles by Alfonso Sastre.

Drama y sociedad. Madrid: Ediciones Taurus, 1956.

Anatomía del realismo. Barcelona: Ediciones Seix Barral, S.A., 1965.

La revolución y la crítica de la cultura. 2nd Ed. Barcelona: Ediciones Grijalbo, S.A., 1971.

"Autocrítica", of La mordaza. Teatro español 1954-55. Ed. Sainz de Robles. Madrid: Aguilar, 1956, p. 31.

"Espacio-Tiempo y Drama." Primer Acto, No. 6 (enero-febrero 1958), pp. 13-16.

133

"Sobre lo exótico deldrama." Primer Acto, No. 7 (marzo-
abril 1959), pp. 50-52.

"Los espectáculos terribles." Primer Acto, No 8 (mayo-
junio 1959), p. 11.

"Brindis por Anna Christie." Primer Acto, No. 9 (julio-
agosto 1959), pp. 7-9.

"No entienden de teatro." Primer Acto, No. 10 (septiem-
bre-octubre 1959), pp. 2-3.

"Catorce años." Primer Acto, No. 11 (noviembre-diciembre 1959), pp. 1-2.

"Primeras notas para un encuentro con Bertolt Brecht."
Primer Acto, No. 13 (marzo-abril 1960), pp. 11-16.

"Teatro imposible y pacto social." Primer Acto, No. 14
(mayo-junio 1960), pp. 1-2.

"A modo de respuesta," Primer Acto, No. 16 (septiembre-
octubre 1960), pp. 1-2.

"Declaración del G.T.R." Primer Acto, No. 16 (septiem-
bre-octubre 1960), p. 45.

"Teatro de la realidad." Primer Acto, No. 18 (diciem-
bre 1960), pp. 1-2.

"Ni viejos ni jóvenes: todo lo contrario." Primer
Acto, No. 19 (enero 1961), pp. 2-3.

"Problemas dentro y fuera del Tintero." Primer Acto,
No. 20 (febrero 1961), pp. 3-4.

"G.T.R. Primera temporada." Primer Acto, No. 23, (mayo
1961), pp. 12-18.

"Autocrítica", of La cornada. Teatro Español 1959-60.
Ed. Sainz de Robles. Madrid: Aguilar, 1961,
p. 163.

"Autocrítica", of En la red. Teatro español 1960-61.
Ed. Sainz de Robles. Madrid: Aguilar, 1962,
p. 249.

"Subvenciones." Teatro. Madrid: Ediciones Taurus,
1964. pp. 79-80.

"El T.A.S. por última vez." Teatro. Madrid:
Ediciones Taurus, 1964. pp. 81-87.

"Sobre las formas sociales del drama." Teatro. Madrid:
Ediciones Taurus, 1964. pp. 88-94.

"Bibliografía." Teatro. Madrid: Ediciones Taurus, 1964.
pp. 127-136.

"Encuesta sobre la censura." Primer Acto, No. 165,
(enero 1974), pp. 4-5.

Secondary Sources

Anderson, Farris. Alfonso Sastre. New York: Twayne
Publishers Inc., 1971.

_____. "The New Theatre of Alfonso Sastre."
Hispania, 55, 4 (December 1972), 840-47.

Anon. "Teatro en toda España: Sastre, Muñoz Seca y
Robert Thomas." Primer Acto, No 21 (marzo 1961),
p. 61.

Anon. "Alfonso Sastre." España, Hoy, No. 16 (octubre
1971), p. 48.

Anon. "Preguntas a los autores." Primer Acto, No. 131
(abril 1971), pp. 11-15.

Aub, Max. "Prólogo acerca del teatro español de los
años veinte de este siglo." Cuadernos Americanos,
24, 140 (mayo-junio 1965), 194-210.

Benedikt, Michael and George E. Wellwarth, Ed. Modern
Spanish Theatre. New York: E.P. Dutton and Co.
Inc., 1968.

_____. Modern Spanish Drama. New York: E.P.
Dutton and Co., Inc., 1969.

Bergamín, José. "Crítica" of La cornada. Teatro
español 1959-60. Ed. Sainz de Robles. Madrid:
Aguilar, 1961, pp. 168-70.

Bilyeu, Elbert E. "Alfonso Sastre: An Analysis of his
Dramas through 1960." Diss. University of Colorado,
1968.

Buero Vallejo, Antonio. "Obligada precisión acerca
  del imposibilismo." Primer Acto, No. 15 (julio-
  agosto 1960), pp. 1-6.

Casali, Renzo. "Bertolt Brecht." Primer Acto, No. 90
  (noviembre 1967), pp. 63-64.

Castellano, Juan R. "Los premios nacionales de teatro
  en España." Hispania, 38, 3 (September 1955),
  291-93.

_____. "¿Está en crisis el teatro español?"
  Cuadernos Americanos, 17, 2 (marzo-abril 1958),
  237-44.

_____. "Estado actual del teatro español."
  Hispania, 41, 4 (December 1958), 431-35.

Chantraine de Van Pragg, Jacqueline. "Alfonso Sastre:
  la esperanza del joven teatro español." La Torre,
  Año 10, 40 (October-December 1962), 111-19.

Clocchiatti, Emilio. "España y su teatro contemporáneo."
  Insula, Año 19, 206 (enero 1964), n. pag.

Corrigan, Robert W., Ed. The New Theatre of Europe.
  New York: Dell Publishing Co. Inc., 1962.

_____. "Masters of the Modern Theatre."
  Masterpieces of the Modern Spanish Theatre. New
  York: The Macmillan Co. 1967, pp. 11-29.

De Coster, Cyrus C. "The Theatrical Season in Madrid
  1954-1955." Hispania, 39, 2 (May 1956), 182-85.

_____. "Alfonso Sastre." Tulane Drama
  Review, (December, 1960), pp. 121-32.

_____. "Two recent plays by Alfonso
  Sastre." Hispania, 44, 44 (December 1961), 758.

De la Torre, Claudio. "Montaje de El cuervo." Primer
  Acto, No. 6 (enero-febrero 1958), p. 20.

Domenech, Ricardo. "Primer encuentro con el drama de
  acción social." Primer Acto, No. 8 (mayo-junio
  1959), pp. 6-10.

_____. "Notas sobre teatro." Cuadernos
  Hispanoamericanos, 2, 128-129 (agosto-septiembre

1960), 251-58.

_____. "Los jóvenes en el teatro: El movi-
miento se demuestra andando." Primer Acto, No. 17
(noviembre 1960), pp. 2-3.

_____. "Teatro en toda España." Primer Acto,
No. 22 (abril 1961), pp. 2-4.

_____. "Tres obras de un autor revolucion-
ario." Teatro. Madrid: Ediciones Taurus, 1964.
pp. 37-47.

_____. "Entrevista con Alfonso Sastre."
Teatro. Madrid: Ediciones Taurus, 1964. pp. 56-62.

_____. "Lo nuevo y lo viejo en el teatro
social. La nueva literatura dramática: sentido
de su lucha." Primer Acto, No. 54 (julio 1964),
pp. 14-16.

_____. "Notas de bibliografía teatral."
Cuadernos Hispanoamericanos, No. 233 (mayo 1969),
pp. 467-77.

Donahue, Francis. "Spain's Theater of Commitment."
Books Abroad 43, 3 (Summer 1969), 354-58.

Fernán Gómez, Fernando, Alfonso Paso, Conrado Blanco.
"Problemas del teatro español." Primer Acto, No. 13
(marzo-abril 1959), pp. 3-10.

Fernández Santos, Angel. "Oficio de tinieblas de
Alfonso Sastre." Insula Año 22, 244 (marzo 1967),
17.

Ferrer, Olga Prjevalinsky. "Three Years of Spanish
Theater: 1960-63." Books Abroad 38, 1 (Winter
1964), 28-31.

García-Abrines, Luis. "La poesía accidental en el
teatro de Sastre." Duquesne Hispanic Review, 1,
1 (1962), 41-50.

García Escudero, José María. "Tiempo." Teatro. Madrid:
Ediciones Taurus, 1964, pp. 65-69.

García Pavón, F. El teatro social en España. Madrid:
Ediciones Taurus, 1962.

Garzo, Eugenio: "El teatro de Alfonso Sastre." Cuadernos Hispanoamericanos, No. 59 (noviembre 1954),
pp. 213-215.

Giuliano, William. Buero Vallejo, Sastre y el teatro
de su tiempo. New York: Las Americas Pub. Co.,
Inc., 1971.

Gómez García, Manuel. "Así piensan 40 profesionales
de nuestra escena sobre censura, teatro social y
teatro político en España." Primer Acto, No. 131
(abril 1971), pp. 13-14.

González, Emilio. "La obra dramática de Alfonso Sastre."
Revista Hispánica Moderna, 27. 3-4 (1961), 333.

Halfitter, Cristóbal. "La música de La cornada." Primer
Acto. No. 12 (enero-febrero 1960), p. 26.

Haro Tecglen, Eduardo. "Introducción a Alfonso Sastre."
Primer Acto. No. 6 (enero-febrero 1958), pp. 16-19.

Holt, Marion. Ed. The Modern Spanish Stage: Four Plays.
New York: Hill and Wang, 1970.

Marqueríe, Alfredo. "Crítica" of La mordaza. Teatro
español 1954-55. Ed. Sainz de Robles. Madrid:
Aguilar, 1956, pp. 33-35.

Marsillach, Adolfo. "Cuaderno de dirección de La
cornada." Primer Acto, No. 12 (enero-febrero 1960),
pp. 17-26.

Martínez Ruiz, Florencio. "El último teatro realista
español." Papeles de Son Armadans, 45, 133 (abril
1967), 177-192.

Merchant, Moelwyn. "The irony of Bertolt Brecht."
Man in the Modern Theatre. Ed. Nathan A. Scott, Jr.
Richmond, Virginia: John Knox Press, 1965. pp. 58-
75.

Monleón, José. "Reflexión sobre sesenta títulos."
Primer Acto, No. 11 (noviembre-diciembre 1959),
pp. 41-44.

_____. "Crítica" of En la red. Teatro
español 1960-61. Ed. Sainz de Robles. Madrid:
Aguilar, 1962, pp. 254-57.

_____. "Teatro en Madrid." Primer Acto,
No. 21 (marzo 1961), pp. 40-43.

_____. Treinta años de teatro de la derecha.
Barcelona: Tusquets Editor, 1971.

Nerva, Sergio. "Crítica" of La mordaza. Teatro español
1954-55. Ed. Sainz de Robles. Madrid: Aguilar,
1956, pp. 35-38.

_____. "Crítica" of En la red. Teatro
español 1960-61. Ed. Sainz de Robles. Madrid:
Aguilar, 1962, pp. 252-254.

O'Connor, Patricia W. "Government Censorship in the
Contemporary Spanish Theatre." Educational Theater
Journal, 18, 4 (December 1966). 443-49.

_____. "Censorship in the Contemporary
Spanish Theater and Antonio Buero Vallejo."
Hispania, 52, 2 (May 1969), 282-88.

Pablo, Luis de. "La música concreta necesaria." Primer
Acto, No. 12 (enero-febrero 1960), p. 16.

Pasquariello, Anthony M. "Alfonso Sastre y Escuadra
hacia la muerte." Hispanófila, 5, 15 (May 1962),
57-63.

_____. "Censorship in the Spanish Theatre
and Alfonso Sastre's The Condemned Squad." Theatre
Annual, 19 (1962), 19-26.

_____. "Alfonso Sastre: Dramatist in
Search of a Stage." Theatre Annual, 22 (1965-66),
16-23.

_____. "Dramatist with a Mission." Escuadra
hacia la muerte. New York: Appleton-Century-Crofts,
1967. pp. 1-8.

Pemán, José María. "La cornada." Primer Acto, No. 12
(enero-febrero 1960), pp. 12-15.

Pérez Minik, Domingo. "Se trata de Alfonso Sastre,
dramaturgo melancólico de la Revolución." Teatro.
Madrid: Ediciones Taurus, 1964, pp. 11-36.

_____. "Prólogo" Alfonso Sastre Obras Com-
pletas 1. Madrid: Aguilar, 1967. pp. ix-xxxi.

139

Ponce, Fernando. Introducción al teatro contemporáneo.
   Madrid: Editora Nacional, 1969.

Posada, Francisco. Lukács, Brecht y la situación actual
   del realismo socialista. Buenos Aires: Editorial
   Galerna, 1969.

Prego, Adolfo. "Crítica" of La cornada. Teatro español
   1959-60. Ed. Sainz de Robles. Madrid: Aguilar,
   1961, pp. 165-168.

_____. "Crítica" of En la red. Teatro español
   1960-61. Ed. Sainz de Robles. Madrid: Aguilar, 1962,
   pp. 249-52.

Pronko, Leonard C. "The 'Revolutionary Theatre' of
   Alfonso Sastre." Tulane Drama Review, 5, 2 (December 1960), 111-132.

Quinto, José María de. "Un nuevo sentido de la kárthar-
   sis." Primer Acto, No. 22 (abril 1961), pp. 4-5.

_____. "Breve historia de una lucha." Teatro.
   Madrid: Ediciones Taurus, 1964. pp. 48-55.

Richardson, Ruth. "Algunos datos sobre dramaturgos
   españoles contemporáneos." Homenaje a Federico de
   Onís (1885-1966), Revista Hispánica Moderna, 34,
   (1968), 413-23.

Rodríguez Puértolas, J. "Tres aspectos de una misma
   realidad en el teatro español contemporáneo:
   Buero, Sastre, Olmo." Hispanófila, 11, 31 (1967),
   43-58.

Sainz de Robles, Federico Carlos. Teatro español 1959-
   60. Madrid: Aguilar, 1961. pp. xiv-xv.

Santos, Angel.Fernández. "Crónica de teatro." Insula,
   24, 277 (1969), 15.

Schwartz, Kessel. "Tragedy and the Criticism of Alfonso
   Sastre". Symposium. 21, 4 (Winter 1967), 338-46.

_____. "Posibilismo and Imposibilismo:
   The Buero Vallejo-Sastre Polemic." Homenaje a
   Federico de Onís (1885-1966), Revista Hispánica
   Moderna, 34, (1968) 436-45.

_____. The Meaning of Existence in Contemporary Hispanic Literature. Coral Gables, Florida: University of Miami Press, 1969.

Seator, Lynette H. "A Study of the Plays of Alfonso Sastre: A Man's Struggle for Identity in a Hostile World." Diss. University of Illinois, 1972.

Server, Alberta W. "Notes on the Contemporary Drama in Spain." Hispania, 42, 1 (March 1959), 56-60.

Soldevila, Ignacio Durante. "Sobre el teatro español de los últimos veinticinco años." Cuadernos Americanos, 22, 1 (enero-febrero 1963), 256-89.

Torrente Ballester, Gonzálo. "Crítica" of La mordaza. Teatro español 1954-55. Ed. Sainz de Robles. Madrid: Aguilar, 1956, pp. 31-33.

_____. "Crítica" of La cornada. Teatro español 1959-60. Ed. Sainz de Robles. Madrid: Aguilar, 1961, pp. 163-65.

_____. Panorama de la literatura española. 1. Madrid: Ediciones Guadarrama, 1961, pp. 465-66.

_____. Teatro español contemporáneo. 2nd ed. Madrid: Ediciones Guadarrama, 1968.

Valbuena Prat, Angel. Teatro moderno español. Zaragoza: Ediciones Partenón, 1944.

_____. Historia del teatro español. Barcelona: Editorial Noguer, 1956.

Van der Naald, Anje C. Alfonso Sastre: Dramaturgo de la revolución. New York: Las Americas Publishing Co. Inc., 1973.

Vázquez Zamora, Rafael. "Un estreno y un reestreno: La mordaza de Alfonso Sastre." Insula, Año 11, 106 (octubre 1954), p. 12.

_____. "Autores de hoy y mañana: Alfonso Sastre." Insula, Año 12, 130 (septiembre 1957), 10.

_____. "La actualidad teatral: El cuervo de Alfonso Sastre en el María Guerrero." Insula, Año 12, 132 (noviembre 1957), 11.

_____. "La cornada de Alfonso Sastre en el Lara." Insula, Año 15, 159 (febrero 1960), 15.

_____. "Alfonso Sastre no acepta el 'posibilismo'." Insula, Año 15, 164-165 (1960) 27.

_____. "Un mes de teatro: En la red de Alfonso Sastre." Insula, Año 16, 173 (1961), 15.

Villegas, Juan. "La sustancia metafísica de la tragedia y su función social: Escuadra hacia la muerte de Alfonso Sastre'" Symposium, 21, 3 (Fall 1967), 255-63.

Webber, Edwin J. "The 'Problem' of the Spanish Theatre Today." Hispania, 39, 1 (March 1956), 63-67.

Wellwarth, George E. "Introduction." The New Wave Spanish Drama. New York: New York University Press, 1970, ix-xviii.

_____. The Theatre of Protest and Paradox. New York: New York University Press, 1971.

_____. Spanish Underground Drama. University Park, Pennsylvania: Pennsylvania State University Press, 1972.

APPENDIX

A chronological list of Alfonso Sastre's plays
and the dates of their performance in Spain.[1]

1945	Ha sonado la muerte	Performed in	1946
1946	Uranio 235		1946
1946	Cargamento de sueños	-	1948
*1947	Comedia sonámbula		
*1950	Prólogo patético		
*1951	El cubo de la basura		
1952	Escuadra hacia la muerte		1953
1953	El pan de todos		1957
1954	La mordaza		1954
*1954	Tierra roja		
*1955	Ana Kleiber		
1955	La sangre de Dios		1955
*1955	Muerte en el barrio		
*1955	Guillermo Tell tiene los ojos tristes		
1956	El cuervo		1957
1958	Medea (adaptation of Euripedes)		1958
1959	Asalto nocturno		
1959	En la red		1961
1959	La cornada		1960
1960	Los acreedores (adaptation of Strindberg)		1962
*1960	La dama del mar (adaptation of Ibsen)		
1962	Oficio de tinieblas		1967

*1962 El circulito de tiza (a play for children)

1963 Mulato (adaptation of Langston Hughes)   1963

1965 La sangre y la ceniza (not published)

1965 El banquete (not published)

1966 Marat-Sade (adaptation of Weiss)   1968

1966 La taberna fantástica (not published)

1968 Crónicas romanas (not published)

1969 Rosas rojas para mí (adaptation of Sean O'Casey)
                                             1969

1969 Los secuestrados de Altona (adaptation of Sartre)
                                             1972

1970 Ejercicios de terror (not published)

1971 Asalto de la ciudad (adaptation of Lope de Vega,
                                      not published)

1971 Las cintas magnéticas (not published)

1971 Askatasuna (not published)

1971 El camarada oscuro (not published)

---

[1]This list was compiled from a bibliography given to the author by Alfonso Sastre.

*According to Alfonso Sastre these published works (indicated with an asterisk) have not been performed in Spain. Almost all of them have been prohibited because of censorship in the theatre.

About the author

The author Dr. T. Avril Bryan was born in Port-of-Spain, Trinidad where she received her early education. She attended Sheffield University, England where she obtained a B.A. degree in Spanish, French and Latin. Dr. Bryan then attended the University of Nebraska-Lincoln, U.S.A. where she studied for the M.A. and Ph.D. in Spanish. She has been the author of several articles on Spanish Literature and on Spanish linguistics. This is her first full length monograph. She has been on the faculty at the University of Nebraska-Lincoln and the University of Rhode Island as well as a Visiting Lecturer at Indiana University in Bloomington. In 1976 Dr. Bryan returned to Trinidad where she has been Lecturer at the University of the West Indies in St. Augustine.